The Extent and Efficacy

of the

Life and Work

of Jesus Christ

James A. Fowler

C.I.Y. Publishing
P.O. Box 1822
Fallbrook, CA 92088-1822

THE EXTENT AND EFFICACY
OF THE LIFE AND WORK OF JESUS CHRIST

Revised Second Edition

Copyright ©2013 by James A. Fowler

Published by C.I.Y. Publishing
P.O. Box 1822
Fallbrook, California 92088-1822

Printed in the United States of America

ISBN – 978-1-929541-45-4

TABLE OF CONTENTS

PREFACE

To the Revised Second Edition

The first edition of this book elicited many responses, both of agreement and disagreement. It was encouraging that people were reading the content of the book and discussing the biblical and theological implications of what was written.

Whereas the first edition was rushed into print to provide a text of the teaching that was delivered at the Dan Stone Memorial Conference in Dalton, Pennsylvania on Memorial Day weekend, 2012, this revised second edition seeks to remove the spoken elements of the original text. The basic textual content of the first edition is retained, but the latter portion of the message was directed more specifically to the audience assembled at the conference. It is that latter portion that has been rewritten to provide a more generic conclusion to the dialectic proposed in this document.

In that there was some misunderstanding of the dialectic contrast of the objective-universal and subjective-particular, additional addenda have been added that provide explanation for questions that were asked. (*Addenda S – V*).

James A. Fowler
February, 2013

THE EXTENT AND EFFICACY
OF THE LIFE AND WORK OF JESUS CHRIST

DIAGRAM:

The reader is advised to view the dialectic diagram that graphically depicts the structure of the thoughts contained in this article. It should be consulted regularly throughout the reading of this article in order to keep perspective on the author's flow of thought. (*cf. Addendum A and B*)

ABSTRACT:

The extent and efficacy of the life and work of Jesus Christ is best viewed in the context of a balanced tension of a both/and dialectic between the objective-universal "all" of humanity at large and the subjective-particular wherein "not all" will choose to individually and personally respond to Jesus Christ. Over-emphasis on the subjective-particular that diminishes or denies the objective-universal leads to aberrant extremisms of particularism, either objective particularism or subjective particularism. Over-emphasis on the objective-universal that diminishes or denies the subjective-particular leads to extremisms of universalism, either general universalism or deterministic universalism.

Introduction

In theological discussions of the past this study would likely have been entitled "The Extent and Efficacy of the Atonement," as the work of Christ has traditionally been focused on the redemptive work of the Paschal Lamb on the cross of Calvary. The apostle Paul explicitly stated that he "determined not to know anything among (*the Corinthians*), save Jesus Christ, and him crucified" (I Cor. 2:2), and affirmed, "we preach Christ crucified" (I Cor. 1:23). The death of Jesus Christ on the cross has thus often been the central focus of Christian theological discussions explicating how the blood of the divine-human Lamb of God was shed for the sins of mankind in likeness unto the blood of the sacrificial lamb slain for the sins of the Hebrew peoples in the old covenant on the Day of Atonement (*Yom Kippur*).

The word "atonement," a word long used in theological discussion, is somewhat of a *hapax logomena*, a singular occurrence of a theological word deriving from English origin. The Middle English adverbial phrase, *at oon* (meaning "at one"), was the etymological source of the English words "atone" and "atonement," used to refer to the reconciliation of estranged parties in the *at-one-ment* of unified relationship.

Theologically this was applied to the estrangement of God and sinful mankind with the recognition that "God was in Christ, reconciling the world to Himself" (II Corinthians 5:19). For "it was the Father's good pleasure...through Him (Jesus Christ), to reconcile all things to Himself, having made peace through the blood of the cross..." (Col. 1:19,20). The grace of God effected redemption in Christ Jesus when God the Father allowed His Son, to be publicly displayed in death on a cross as the propitiation (expiation, satisfaction) in His blood for the estrangement of sin (cf. Rom. 3:24,25). "He is the propitiation for our sins; and not for ours only, but also for those of the whole world" (I John 2:2).

But the work of Christ did not commence or conclude with His death on the cross, and must not be limited to the redemptive implications of His crucifixion and atoning sacrifice. The early Greek Fathers of the

Church recognized that the work of Christ must include the ramifications of the incarnation when the Son of God became flesh (cf. Jn. 1:14), both God and man, the "one mediator between God and man, the man Christ Jesus" (I Tim. 2:5). The incarnational enfleshment of the second person of the Godhead was regarded as an important component of the atoning work of the divine-human Redeemer. Gregory of Nazianzus explained the pivotal importance of the incarnation when he wrote, "That which was not assumed is not healed; but that which is united to God is saved." (*Epistle 51 to Cledonius; Ep. 101, 32: SC 208, 50*) The reconciling work of at-one-ment could only heal the estrangement of God and man via the incarnated God-man, who could thus be the representative sacrifice on man's behalf. It should even be noted that the work of Christ began prior to the historic incarnation when the pre-existent Son of God "did not regard equality with God a thing to be grasped, but emptied Himself, taking the form of a bond-servant, being made in the likeness of men" (Phil. 2:6,7).

An even broader perspective recognizes that the atoning work of Christ extends beyond the historical incarnation and redemptive sacrifice of crucifixion, allowing a complete and comprehensive theological concept of atonement to include the work of Christ from pre-existence through post-ascension. Christ's atoning endeavors go even beyond His birth, death, and resurrection as He continues to "draw all men to Himself" (John 12:32), and continues to engage in the atoning work of intercession (Heb. 7:25; I John 2:1) within His "permanent priesthood" (Heb. 7:24) on behalf of all mankind.

Having thus explained the expansion of the title beyond usual considerations of atonement, we proceed to consider the extent and efficacy of the comprehensive work of Jesus Christ in the historical past, in the experiential present, and in the expected future.

How extensive, how inclusive, how effective is the life and work of Jesus Christ? What we are dealing with in this study is the basic premises of the entire Christian faith: The importance of the incarnation of the Son of God when "the Word became flesh" (Jn. 1:14) in the hypostatic union of deity and humanity; the means by which Jesus lived the life that He lived "without sin" (II Cor. 5:21); the humiliating sacrifice whereby Jesus undeservedly submitted Himself to die, "even death on a cross" (Phil. 2:8); the purpose of His death "as a ransom for many" (Matt. 20:28), for "all" (I Tim. 2:6); the objective of His death, burial, resurrection and ascension in order that human beings might have spiritual life (Jn. 10:10); and the individual response to His life and work when people ask, "What must we do to be saved?" (Acts 2:38; 16:30). These are basic fundamentals of the Christian faith.

This study is a comprehensive consideration of the life and work of Jesus Christ, both in His objective and historical manifestation as well in the on-going subjective and experiential function of the risen and living Lord Jesus. For whom did the Son of God become the God-man, who lived perfectly, and died by Roman crucifixion, and rose from the dead on the third day, and ascended into heaven, and was poured out on Pentecost. Was **who** Jesus was (and is) and **what** Jesus did (and does) in His "finished work" effective for all human persons, unreservedly, or does the effectiveness of the life and work of Jesus have to be qualified in some form of limitation?

The parameters of this study are a "big bite to chew," but it is important to try to grasp the "big picture" of the gospel. In an attempt to see this "big picture," we will again be utilizing one of the dialectic diagrams that I have become known for. It will illustrate the paradoxical contrasts inherent in this broad topic.

The dialectics of Christian thought involve two seemingly contradictory or opposing ideas that are both biblical tenets and must be held in tensioned balance one to the other. The contrasts do not pose a polarized *either/or* dichotomy, but rather a *both/and* tension in which the two tenets may appear to be in conflict, but must always be maintained in a complementary balance. To emphasize either tenet to the diminishment, neglect or denial of the other is to veer off into aberrant teaching that is no longer in accord with biblically balanced thinking. Those extremist positions are then juxtaposed into dichotomist or dualist either/or contrasts that have long been the basis of theological conflict.

The delicate tight-rope procedure of dialectic thinking does not come easy to the Western mind-set of Aristotelian methodology, that seeks to eliminate the tensions in a reductionism of one tenet by the elevation and predominant emphasis of the other tenet, seeking to get every issue of thought figured out, nailed down, systematized, and fully explained without loose ends. In order to avoid such reductionism, we will be forced to "think outside the box," outside of the "comfort zone" parameters of our traditional and popular traditions of Christian interpretation and understanding.

Those who want air-tight categories or boxes of absolute thought and doctrine will often view dialectic thought suspiciously as a form of relativism, but the relative factor of dialectic thinking is simply that one truth tenet must always be viewed relative to the other, and in conjunction with the other. The dialectic thought herein proposed does not entail the relativizing of one tenet to establish the supremacy of the other.

In the topic under consideration, we will deal with two absolutely biblical truth-tenets that must be held in tensioned balance. Both are equally valid. Both are equally biblical.

In previous teaching I have used the dialectic between the objective and the subjective. The objective, you might remember, is that which is *outside* of us, and the subjective is that which is *inside* of us. The objective is *external* to us. The subjective is *internal* within us. We will be considering another dialectic at the same time. This will be the dialectic between the universality and the particularity of the extent and effect of the life and work of Jesus Christ – How the life and work of Jesus has universal effect for all mankind from an objective perspective, but at the same time has a particularized effect on some individuals and not on others, based on the subjective response of those persons.

So, the two poles of the dialectic we are considering involve: (*cf. Addendum C*)

- **The objective-universal**
- **The subjective-particular**

This dialectic distinction I am drawing between the objective-universal and the subjective-particular goes back at least as far as the philosophy of Georg Wilhelm Friedrich Hegel (1770-1831). (*cf. Addendum D*) Hegel, you might remember, was a German philosopher known for his method of dialectic, but he did not advocate balanced tension of the dialectic tenets, for he was always seeking to take the *thesis* and the *antithesis* and merge them together in a *synthesis* that then became another thesis so that human reason could boil down all thought into bottom-line truth statements. When I began to search for previous instances of this dialectic that I am using between "objective universal" and "subjective particular" I discovered that Hegel had used these categories in his theory of marriage, contrasting marriage as both a natural relation (a physical and legal bond of union) as well as an ethical relationship (a psychological and spiritual bond of union). The natural relations of the objective/universal side of marriage involves human parties as differentiated entities bound together legally and physically, i.e. the two become one. The ethical relations of the subjective/particular side of marriage involves human individuals in a mutual, whole-hearted surrender of individual personality (the love that gives oneself up for the other). Hegel's philosophy was heavily weighted toward the objective/universal of dialectic syllogisms. He was quite anti-individualistic (even impersonal) in his thought, and said concerning the subjective/particular side of the marital love-relationship, "What develops between these individuals may indeed be of infinite importance to *them*, but it is of no significance whatever in itself," (*Philosophy of Right*, 167). Hegelian philosophy does not give much credence to the "subjective particular" of what transpires within individuals. That, by the way, was the driving force of Soren Kierkegaard's philosophical works, to debunk Hegel's emphasis on the "objective universal" to establish absolute truth tenets, by emphasizing the individual response of the "subjective particular," even going so far as to say, "truth is subjectivity."

We want to consider how the objective-universal and the subjective-particular apply to the life and work of Jesus Christ and the relationship those who receive Him as Christians have with the living Lord Jesus.

First, the **objective universal** that asserts that **ALL** of humanity is included in the extent and efficacy of the "finished work" of Jesus Christ. Who Jesus was (and is) and what Jesus did (and does) is effective for every human person who has ever lived, continues to live, and will ever live.

Second, the **subjective particular** asserts that **NOT ALL** human beings desire to participate in the life and work of Jesus Christ. As human beings they have the freedom of choice to either **receive** what is available in Jesus Christ or to **reject** what is available in Jesus Christ.

To begin with we will focus on these two poles – the **objective universal of the ALL** and the **subjective particular of the NOT ALL**, explaining that the life and work of Jesus Christ is effective for (1) **all** of humanity and (2) **not all** of humanity. These two positions would be logically contradictory and incapable of interacting as equally valid truth-tenets, if they were not both stated explicitly in the scriptures as part of the Theo-logic of God's purposes. Isa. 55:8,9 – "My thoughts are not your thoughts, nor are your ways My ways," declares the Lord. "For as the heavens are higher than the earth, so are My ways higher than your ways, and My thoughts than your thoughts."

The place where we must begin is not with the human logic of philosophical theology, but with the biblical evidence that will document the veracity of the two categories we have placed side by side in this dialectic. Intellectual fairness demands that we begin by establishing the biblical paradigm with its contrasting documentable statements prior to attempting to show various systems of theological thought that are outside of those parameters.

      We will eventually go on to explain that the columns on the outside of these two poles of the dialectic represent the aberrations that result when the two tenets of the dialectic are not kept in balanced tension. Whenever one position is emphasized to the neglect, diminishment or denial of the other an extremism of overemphasis results that absolutizes one perspective into a misguided system of thought – a man-made ...ism. You will notice (when we get there) that the outside columns are replete with many ...isms. (*cf. Addendum E*)

Objective Universal

As we begin to consider the objective universal of God's action in Jesus Christ, it is important to note that an objective reality is true whether we believe it or not! These are enacted by God outside of us, and we have no part in the effecting of them. They are not contingent upon our consent or cooperation.

God, by His GRACE that was "realized in Jesus Christ" (John 1:17), took the initiative to unilaterally enact certain spiritual realities with universal significance for "all the world," for "all men" (sometimes referred to in scripture as "the many" – as opposed to the particular "few"). God, in the Self-revealing of Himself in His Son, acted on behalf of every fallen human person to redeem, reconcile and restore ALL mankind to Himself.

The following survey of objective/subjective truth tenets (*cf. Addendum F*) are not to be construed as necessarily indicative of any particular theological group or movement. It was compiled simply by considering the New Testament statements referring to the comprehensive "ALL" statement that can (and have) been utilized within church history to explain the objective/subjective perspective of Christ's life and work. The inclusion of these various interpretations is not intended to serve as a blanket advocacy or espousal of the interpretations of these points, and it must be admitted that the scriptural citations used to document some positions will not be considered hermeneutically viable or accurate by some readers.

• We begin with the objective universal fact that *ALL humanity is **loved** by God in Christ*. And we turn to the most basic, well-known scripture verse, "God so loved the world (of fallen mankind), that He gave His only begotten Son..." That is the objective universal part. The rest of the verse falls in the other column of the subjective particular: "...that whoever believes in Him shall not perish but have eternal life." "God so loved the world, that He gave His only begotten Son...," that is an objective universal reality whether you (or I) believe it or not! But if we believe it, i.e. receive HIM, then the subjective particular will be realized, in that you "will not perish, but have eternal life" (The particulars of an either-or). The next verse, John 3:17, reads, "For God did not send the Son into the world to judge the world (of fallen humanity), but that the world (objective universal of all mankind) might (should) be saved through Him." Then, John 3:18 comes back to the subjective particular side of the dialectic: "He who believes in Him is not judged; he who does not believe has been judged already, because he has not believed in the name of the only begotten Son of God." (a particularizing of believer and unbeliever; not judged and judged).

The objective universal of God's love for all mankind in Jesus Christ is further documented by Romans 5:18 – "God demonstrates His love toward us (all mankind), in that while we were yet sinners, Christ died for us." I John 4:10 – "In this is love, not that we loved God (subjective particular), but that He loved us (objective universal) and sent His Son to be the propitiation for our sins." Propitiation has to do with "satisfaction." God is satisfied that Jesus Christ has done everything necessary in His life and death to deal with and counteract and overcome all of the sins of all human persons. (cf. Eph. 2:4; II Thess. 2:16; Rev. 1:5)

16

• Correlative to the gospel announcement that ALL humanity is loved by God in Christ, it is additionally explained that *ALL humanity is extended mercy in Jesus Christ* (Rom. 11:32) and **graced** *by God in Christ.* Grace is the action of God to reach out to others in love, expressing and Self-revealing the Being of His own character of Love (I Jn. 4:8,16) through the being and action of the Son, Jesus Christ. John's gospel explains (1:17), "Grace was realized through Jesus Christ." We could further amplify by noting that Grace is realized and expressed *sola Christos*, in Jesus Christ alone.

From eternity past God has purposed to act in grace toward all humanity in His Son, Jesus Christ. Paul writes to Timothy that by "the power of God … according to His own purpose and *grace* which was granted us in Christ Jesus from all eternity, and now has been revealed by the appearing of our Savior Jesus Christ" (II Tim. 1:9), we have the privilege of participating in the gospel. Then to Titus, Paul writes, "the *grace* of God has appeared, bringing salvation to ALL men" (2:11). ALL of humanity shares in being the recipients and participants of the GRACE of God in Jesus Christ.

- There is a theological camp that declares that only a particular few – NOT ALL – are elect in Christ. There are others who believe that the scripture asserts the objective universal that *ALL humanity is **elected**, selected, and chosen in Christ.* Paul writes in Ephesians 1:4, "He (God, the Father) chose us (all men? Or just Christians) in Him (Jesus Christ) before the foundation of the world, that we should be holy and blameless before Him (God, the Father). 1:5 – "In love He (God) predestined (pre-horizoned) us (all men or just Christians?) to adoption as sons through Jesus Christ to Himself, according to the kind intention of His will, (1:6) to the praise of the glory of His grace, which He freely bestowed on us (all men or just Christians?) in the Beloved."

There is an objective universal sense in which ALL humanity is elected, chosen, determined and predestined (pre-horizoned – based on the Greek word *prohorizo*) to become the elect family of adopted children, the "elect," chosen people of God, by incorporation into the Chosen Son of God, the Elect One, Jesus Christ. God speaks through Isaiah, referring to Jesus Christ, "Behold My Servant whom I uphold, *My*

Chosen One in whom My soul delights" (Isa. 42:1). At the transfiguration God spoke out of the cloud, saying "This is My Son, *My Chosen One*, listen to Him" (Lk. 9:35).

The Reformed Swiss theologian of the 20th century, Karl Barth, is the foremost Christian thinker to have emphasized that the Son, Jesus Christ, is the "Elect One" of God, and that those who are "in Him" ("in Christ") are elect ones in the Elect One. His conclusion was that this includes ALL of humanity in a representative oneness with the divine-human Christ, while others maintain that NOT ALL are elect ones in the Elect One, Jesus. I Peter 2:6 identifies Jesus as the "Elect Stone," the cornerstone (of redeemed humanity), and he who believes in Him (subjective particular) shall not be disappointed." Paul writes to Timothy in II Tim. 2:10, "I endure all things for the sake of those who are chosen (elect – all mankind or just Christians?), that they may obtain the salvation which is in Christ Jesus, and with it eternal glory."

Some readers may want to jump over into the other column (subjective particular) at this point, saying, "Yes ... Christians who have particularized themselves by a subjective choice to receive Jesus are specifically identified as the 'elect of God' (Col. 3:12; I Thess 1:4; I Peter 1:2; II Pet. 1:10; Rev. 17:14)," but for the time being we are considering the objective universal of God's having elected and predestined (pre-horizoned) to save all human beings in, by, and through the "Elect One," His Son, Jesus Christ, prior to, and not contingent upon an individual's response.

• The only begotten Son of God incarnated in the person of Jesus Christ represented all humanity. *ALL humanity is **represented** in solidarity with the Son's becoming the singular God-man with the right and capability to represent every fallen human being* in voluntarily assuming identification with, and the consequences of sin in sacrificial death on their behalf. Do you concur that Jesus Christ represented every individual human person?

Even though we Americans live in a country that has representative government, it is still difficult for many to grasp how one man can represent many (or ALL) and cause the many (ALL) to be drawn into solidarity with him by and with his action. I Cor. 15:22 states, "in Adam all die, so also in Christ will all be made alive." Adam and Christ (the "last Adam") are the two representative men, with whom all the rest of humanity is connected in spiritual representation. That is brought out in stark contrast in Romans 5:15-21 where it is noted that "by the transgression of the one (Adam) the many (ALL) died, ... by the grace of the one Man, Jesus Christ, the gift abounded to the many (ALL). ... from one transgression (Adam's) death reigned ... and condemnation resulted, ... but from the One, Jesus Christ, there results justification and the gift of righteousness to reign in life. Through the one man's disobedience (Adam's) the many (ALL) were made sinners, even so through the obedience of the One (Jesus Christ) the many (ALL) were made righteous." Both Adam and Jesus Christ represented us all.

Isaiah prophesied and recorded (Isa. 53:5-12) that the Messiah would be a suffering servant who would be "crushed for our iniquities" (5), as our representative, for "the Lord caused the iniquity of us ALL to fall on Him" (6). He was to be "rendered as a guilt-offering ...to bear the iniquity of the many" (ALL) (11). He, "Himself would bear the sin of the many (ALL) and intercede (representatively) for their (our) transgressions" (12).

Paul stands in amazement that "He (God, the Father) did not spare His own Son, but delivered Him up for us **all**" (Rom. 8:2). And then in Eph. 5:2 – "Christ loved you and gave Himself up for us, an offering and a sacrifice to God." Hebrews 9:26-28 – "He (Jesus) has been manifested to put away sin by the sacrifice of Himself ... offered once (for ALL) to put away the sins of many (ALL)." The representation of Jesus for us is so clear in II Cor. 5:21 – "He (God) made Him (Jesus) *to be sin on our behalf*, so that we might become the righteousness of God in Him."

Throughout the history of Christian theology this reality of Jesus Christ as our representative has been explained in terms of the vicarious substitutional death of Jesus "on our behalf." Representing ALL men, what happened to Jesus happened to us ALL, in that He acted for, and on behalf of, ALL mankind in taking the death consequences of human sin.

• Particularly, this has been noted in the objective truth that *ALL of fallen humanity **died** in Christ's death.*

We recall that death is the consequence of sin, and the devil, the death-dealer, "having the power of death" (Heb. 2:14) has administered the various forms of death on all those who were represented in Adam's original sin. The sinless One, Jesus Christ, allowed the death-dealer to orchestrate the death of His human, physical body on the cross, totally undeservedly – for it was only we, sinful human beings, who deserved all of the death consequences for sin. Jesus took what we deserved. "Christ died for the ungodly" (ALL of us), while we were yet sinners ... and enemies of God (Rom. 5:6,8,10) Christ died for us (ALL). Christ "became a curse for us" (ALL) (Gal. 3:13) by hanging on the tree (the Cross). "He Himself bore our sins in His body on the cross, so that *we might die* to sin and live to righteousness" (I Peter 2:24). "He was made a little lower than the angels, so that by the grace of God He might taste death for EVERYONE" (Heb. 2:9)

Have you ever faced this question? Where were you when Jesus died? YOU and every other person who has ever lived, now lives, or will ever live were "in Christ." Jesus Christ represented ALL mankind as He died on that cross.

Paul explains to the Galatian Christians, "I have been crucified with Christ..." (Galatians 2:20). When was Christ crucified? ...on the cross of Calvary. When were you crucified? ... on that same cross "in Him." Rom. 6:8 – "we have died with Christ." Col. 3:3 – "you have died, and your life is hidden with Christ in God." II Cor. 5:14 – "One (Jesus Christ) died for ALL, therefore ALL died, and He died for ALL, so that they who live might no longer live for themselves."

In Romans 6:6, Paul explained, "our old man was crucified with Him (Christ)." The old me, the old Jim Fowler who was a "sinner" identified with Adam (Rom. 5:19), and thus identified with "the spirit that works in the sons of disobedience" (Eph. 2:2) – that spiritual identity needed to die. When Jesus was crucified on the cross He took that "old man" to its death. And when He was raised from the dead in resurrection, I was raised to "newness of life" (Rom. 6:4), "alive to God in Christ Jesus" (Rom. 6:11). Our spiritual history is integrally tied to the life and death and resurrection of Jesus Christ – objectively. That is why He became God-man for us, and voluntarily died in the mortality of humanity on our behalf, that the death might be taken and His life given to ALL mankind.

- By the Person and work of Jesus Christ *ALL humanity is **redeemed** in Christ.* The price has been paid for all the consequences of sin and for the total restoration of God and man. That is what redemption means! Jesus declared that He "came to give His life a ransom (redemptive payment of deliverance) for many (ALL)" (Matt. 20:28; Mk. 10:45). The "one mediator between God and man, the man Christ Jesus, gave Himself as a ransom for ALL" (I Tim. 2:5,6). The price was paid to ransom ALL slaves of sin (ALL fallen humanity), to deliver them from that sinful state and restore them to be "man as God intended man to be."

The biblical image of redemption has both a Greek connotation as evidenced in the Greek word *exagorazo*, meaning to "buy out" from the slave market, as well as a Hebrew connotation as portrayed in *gaal*, representing the emancipatory redemption of a kinsman-redeemer. Jesus Christ, the Son of God, by taking on our humanity became the kinsman-redeemer (cf. Ruth 2:20) who would never leave us without a redeemer (cf. Ruth 4:14), but would pay everything necessary to include us in His divine family fellowship.

Every person, every human being, every man, woman, boy and girl, has been redeemed by the death of Jesus Christ. We have "redemption through His blood" (Eph. 1:7). Jesus died to "redeem us (ALL) from the curse" (Gal. 3:13) of sin's consequences, "to redeem us (ALL) from iniquity" (Titus 2:14). We (ALL human beings) have been "bought with a price" (I Cor. 6:20; 7:23). "Through His own blood He entered the Holy Place once for ALL, having obtained eternal redemption" (Heb. 9:12) for all human beings.

When Jesus cried out from the cross, "*Tetelestai,*" "It is finished!" (John 19:30). That is the very Greek word that was written across loan agreements and criminal indictments when the terms were completed, "Paid in full!" The price has been "paid in full" for the redemption and restoration of ALL humanity. This is the universal redemption of mankind. ALL humanity is redeemed in Christ.

• Since the price has been paid in redemption, *ALL humanity is **forgiven** by God in Christ.* The inclusive act of God to acquit, pardon, release and deliver all persons from blame, obligation or guilt seems to proceed to the comprehensive remission of all our sins. There is "no condemnation" (cf. Rom. 8:1) before God.

As Jesus was explaining His mission here on earth He noted that He would bind the strong man, Satan, and then "ALL sins shall be forgiven the sons of man (ALL mankind)" (Mk. 3:28). John the Baptist saw Jesus coming and said, "Behold, the Lamb of God who takes away the sins of the world (ALL fallen, sinful humanity)" (John 1:29).

Paul wrote to the Colossians, "When you were dead in your transgressions and the uncircumcision of your flesh, He (God the Father) made you alive with Him (Jesus Christ), having forgiven us (ALL men) all our transgressions" (Col. 2:13). John's first epistle states, "He Himself (Jesus) is the propitiation (satisfaction) for our sins, and not for ours only, but for those of the whole world (ALL, universal)" (I Jn. 2:2).

How can this be anything but the universal forgiveness of all mankind by the work of Christ? Eph. 1:7 – "In Him we (just Christians? ALL men?) have redemption through His blood, the forgiveness of our trespasses, according to the riches of His grace."

The Episcopal priest, Robert Capon, made this comment: "Who is in heaven? There is nobody in heaven but forgiven sinners because there was nobody available to go to heaven except forgiven sinners. Who is in hell? Hell is occupied by forgiven sinners because there is nobody available to go to hell but forgiven sinners. The difference is that in heaven they *accept* the forgiveness of God in Christ, and in hell they *reject* it." And in that final statement of explanation, Capon points to the subjective particularization of an individual's *acceptance* or *rejection* that does not in any way diminish the objective universal of God's forgiveness of all humanity in Jesus Christ.

• If ALL men are objectively and universally elected, represented, redeemed and forgiven in and by the life and work of Christ, the progression leads to the assertion that *ALL humanity is **reconciled** to (and with) God in Christ.* The estrangement, alienation, and enmity between God and man brought on by the fall of mankind into sin has been settled and resolved by Jesus having taken the consequences of our sin in death.

Romans 5:10,11 – "while we were *enemies* we were *reconciled* to God through the death of His Son, ... through whom we have now received the *reconciliation*."

Colossians 1:19,20 – "It was the Father's good pleasure ... through Him (Jesus) to *reconcile* all things (all mankind) to Himself, having made *peace* through the blood of the cross..." Christ Himself "is our *peace*" (Eph. 2:14).

II Corinthians 5:18-20 – "God *reconciled* us to Himself through Christ and gave us the ministry of *reconciliation*, namely that God was in Christ *reconciling* the world (of fallen humanity) to Himself, not counting their trespasses against them."

The reconciliation between God and mankind has been effected in the death of Jesus Christ. The "period of restoration" (Acts 3:21) has come. The life and work of Jesus Christ restores the relationship between deity and humanity, taking away the alienation and incompatibility of sin and allowing God and man to

be reunited in the concord of reconciled at-one-ment –
yes, union with God through Christ.

Some find this almost incomprehensible and
unbelievable. These affirmations explain the most
awesome realities enacted by God for man. In and by
the incarnation, the crucifixion and resurrection of Jesus
Christ the estranged human race finds objective-
universal peace with God.

• Based on the foregoing it can thereby be asserted
that by the life and work of the Son of God, the divine-
human Jesus, taking away all estrangement and enmity
between God and man, *ALL humanity has been **adopted***
as sons and daughters into the objective and universal
family of God. The whole of humanity is an inclusive
family upon whom God the Father seeks to lavish His
love and blessings and full inheritance.

In his letter to the Galatians, Paul wrote, "God
sent forth His Son, born of a woman, born under the
Law, so that He might redeem those who were under
the Law, that we might receive the *adoption as sons.* ...
Therefore you are no longer a slave, but a son; and if a
son, then an heir through God" (Gal. 4:4-7).

To the Ephesians he explained, "In love He (God) predestined us to *adoption as sons* through Jesus Christ to Himself, according to the kind intention of His will, to the praise of the glory of His grace, which He freely bestowed on us in the Beloved. In Him we have redemption through His blood, the forgiveness of our trespasses, according to the riches of His grace which He lavished on us" (Eph. 1:4-8).

God the Father, through the divine-human Son, has eliminated all estrangement with fallen humanity and accomplished everything necessary to adopt the entire human race as sons and daughters into one big family of God. The social and cultural practices of familial adoption are often patterned after the unilateral adoption of humanity by God in Jesus Christ.

- One step farther in this glorious gospel proclamation: *ALL humanity is **saved** by the life and work of Jesus Christ.*

Paul wrote to young Timothy, "The living God is the Savior of ALL men, especially (particularly) of believers" (I Timothy 4:10). Yes, there is a special subjective and particular spiritual relationship that God has with believers, but the objective and universal truth remains, "The living God is the Savior of ALL men." It's right there in the scripture text.

Then Paul wrote to Titus, "The grace of God has appeared (in Jesus Christ), bringing salvation to ALL men" (Titus 2:11). ... Many of us are so apt to try to qualify these statements to make them say, "The grace of God appeared (in Jesus Christ), bringing the (*opportunity of* or *the availability of*) salvation to all men," or "The grace of God appeared (in Jesus Christ), bringing (*the potential of*) salvation to all men." But such colorized commentary on the text is not valid. The text says directly and explicitly, "The grace of God appeared, bringing *salvation to all men*." Some of us might (and I admit I have done so) attempt to tweak the scripture text with the qualification, "Well, yes, God brought salvation to all men in Christ Jesus, but it only becomes *efficacious* for a person if and when he/she believes." Let us be careful here: the text reads, "The grace of God appeared, *bringing salvation to all men*." Did God fail to "bring salvation to all men" because the human choice of faith counteracts and negates God's action? Are we going to make God's action contingent on man's action? Can any man's action quash the action of God? This kind of thinking begins to set man above God, and effectively denies the scripture text.

Is it not more advisable to accept the text as written, "The grace of God appeared, bringing (actually and absolutely, effectively and efficaciously) salvation to all men," but noting that this is an objective universal reality enacted by God, and for human beings to find personal meaning in such our logical understanding must find a tensioned balance with the subjective particular of an individual's receptivity of faith? (But that is to get ahead of ourselves in the progression of this study.)

The word "salvation" is perhaps the most comprehensive of the terms used for the work of Christ in scripture. Popular usage in modern religious parlance has often made salvation equivalent to conversion or regeneration, and often referred to individuals "getting saved" – which is really non-biblical terminology. The word at the root of all the "salvation" terminology in scripture is the Greek word *sozo* meaning "to make safe." Are not all men *made safe* and delivered from the consequences of sin by the life and death of Jesus

Christ? How can we say otherwise without denying the gospel?

Listen to the apostle John's broad statements: John 3:17 – "God sent His Son into the world that the world (of fallen humanity) might be saved through Him." John 4:42 – the Samaritans responded, "We know for ourselves that this One is the Savior of the world (of fallen humanity)." I John 4:14 – "We have seen and testify that the Father has sent the Son to be the Savior of the world (all men)."

I know that the assertion and advocacy of objective universal salvation – that ALL humanity is saved by God in Christ – is a new perspective for some, but bear with me as I continue this part of the study, and bring out the dialectic balance of the subjective particular in the next section.

• Continuing the objective universal assertions of Christ's life and work, we proceed to note that *ALL humanity has been granted, bequeathed and bestowed with **life** in Jesus Christ.*

The issue in the gospel is life and death, and that is primarily in reference to spiritual life and death. John, in particular, identifies the Son of God, Jesus Christ, with life. "In the beginning was the Word, and the Word was with God, and the Word was God" (Jn. 1:1). He was the "Word of life" (I Jn. 1:1). "In Him was life, and the life was the light of men (ALL men)" (John 1:4). Jesus declared, "I am the way, the truth, and the life" (Jn. 14:6). Is Jesus the "way" only when we subjectively consent to His being the way, or is He the "way" of God whether we believe it or not? Is Jesus the Truth of God only when we personally assent to His being the Truth, or is He the Truth or Reality of God whether we believe it or not? Is Jesus the Life of God only when we receive His life, or is He the Life of God for all mankind even if human beings reject and repudiate His life? Jesus is the objective universal life of God for all mankind.

If Jesus' death is the death of death, and the right of the death-dealer, the devil (Heb. 2:14) is voided and invalidated by Jesus' death, then the only alternative to the objective universal of humanity's spiritual death in Adam is the granting of God's life in Jesus Christ. There is no alternative of a "limbo" between death and life. Death has been taken by Jesus Christ, and we have been given the gift of His life.

Romans 5:18 – "through one transgression (Adam's) there resulted condemnation to all men (objective universal), even so through one act of righteousness (Christ's voluntary submission to death) there resulted justification of **life** to ALL men (objective universal)."

I Corinthians 15:22 – "in Adam ALL die (objective universal), so also in Christ will ALL be made **alive** (objective universal)."

Colossians 2:13 – "when you were dead in your transgressions and the uncircumcision of your heart, He (God the Father) made you **alive** together with Him (Jesus Christ)."

II Timothy 1:10 – God's purpose and grace "have been revealed by the appearing of our Savior, Jesus Christ, who abolished death and brought **life** and immortality to light through the gospel." Were life and immortality brought to light based on our individual acceptance of conversion? Or were life and immortality brought to light in accordance with God's purpose and grace in the gospel of the advent and passion and victory of Jesus Christ? Obviously the latter – the objective universal action of God in Christ.

Please understand that in affirming that ALL humanity is granted and extended the **life** of God in Jesus Christ, this is not the advocacy of "universal regeneration." Regeneration will be considered under the subjective particular of receiving by faith the indwelling life of the risen Lord Jesus in union with one's spirit, when we experience a spiritual exchange that radically changes an individual's spiritual condition. The subjective particularity of spiritual regeneration is not to be confused with the objective-universal of God's granting and extending His life in His Son, Jesus Christ, to all mankind.

• If all humanity has been given life in Jesus Christ, then *ALL humanity has **righteousness** in Christ,* for Paul identifies such as "the righteousness of life" (Rom. 5:18). "Jesus Christ the Righteous" (I John 2:1) has lived and died on our behalf – in identification with all mankind. He was "crushed for our iniquities" (Isa. 53:5), and "the Lord (God the Father) has caused the iniquity of us ALL to fall on Him" (Isa. 53:6). Absorbing our iniquities and unrighteousness, there is "now, therefore, no condemnation" (Rom. 8:1) before God and we are credited with the very righteousness of Christ Himself. We are universally made right with God by the objective work of Christ, but we are adjudged and declared to be righteous in the sight of God in identification with "Jesus Christ, the Righteous." We do not *become* righteous essentially, as only God is, but by what Martin Luther referred to as the "alien righteousness" of Christ, we are regarded as righteous in Christ.

We turn again to Romans 5 where Paul contrasts the objective universal condition of ALL men, both in Adam and in Christ. Romans 5:18,19 – "If by the transgression of the one (Adam) there resulted condemnation to all men (objective universal), even so through the one act of righteousness (Christ's voluntary sacrifice on the cross for the sin of ALL men) there resulted justification (*righteousness*) of life to ALL men (objective universal). Through the one man's disobedience (Adam's) the many (ALL) men were made sinners (objective universal), even so through the obedience of the One (Jesus Christ) the many (ALL) will be made *righteous* (objective universal)."

God does not hold our iniquities and sins against us, but regards ALL humanity as encompassed in the the righteous redemptive actions of the Savior, Jesus Christ, so that we might ALL partake of the *righteousness* that is in Christ. ALL humanity was transferred from the liability column, as it were, to the asset column, from the unrighteous listing to the righteous listing, as it were, in God's books on the basis of the life and work of Jesus Christ.

•   What a blessing has been bestowed upon us ALL in Christ. *ALL humanity is **blessed** by God in Christ.*

In the opening words of Paul's epistle to the Ephesians he wrote, "*Blessed* be the God and Father of our Lord Jesus Christ, who has *blessed* us (ALL? Or just Christians?) with every spiritual *blessing* in the heavenly places in Christ, just as He chose us (ALL?) in Him before the foundation of the world, that we (ALL?) would be holy and blameless before Him. In love He predestined us (ALL?) to adoption as sons through Jesus Christ to Himself, according to the kind intention of His will, to the praise of the glory of His grace, which He freely bestowed on us (ALL?) in the Beloved" (Ephesians 1:3-6).

This verse, like many verses in the new covenant literature, has been exegeted and interpreted both from an objective universal perspective and from a subjective particular perspective. Those who are more prone to apply Paul's words to the blessings that have been given particularly to Christians would point out that this letter is written to the Ephesian Christians ("the saints who are at Ephesus, who are faithful"), and are likely to emphasize that the "spiritual blessings in the heavenly places" are given "in Christ" to those who are particularly and individually "in Christ." The pronouns "us" and "we" they would argue refer only to Christians in particular. Another look might be warranted. Did "He (God) choose us (only Christians?) in Him (Jesus) before the foundation of the world?" Did "He (God) predestine us (only Christians?) to adoption as sons through Jesus Christ?" Did "He (God) freely bestow His grace on us (only Christians?) in the Beloved (Jesus Christ)?" If God's choosing, predestining and bestowal of grace is reserved only for Christians, then one is left with a very Augustinian-Calvinistic perspective of "limited atonement," which is the polarized opposite of the objective universal perspective that we are attempting to document.

Ephesians 1:3 can legitimately be interpreted with a comprehensive explanation that ALL humanity has been (and is) blessed with every spiritual blessing in Christ. Is there any divine blessing that God the Father would withhold from mankind because the life, death and resurrection of Jesus Christ was insufficient to make such available? May it never be!

• Are we suggesting then that ALL men are "in Christ" – representatively "in Him," and "in the Beloved"? Indeed, there is an objective universal sense in which *ALL humanity is "**in Christ**."*

Throughout the scripture record there is an anthropological theme that reveals the solidarity of mankind, wherein the entirety of humanity is united and connected in a corporate oneness, in a common life, identity and destiny. This is particularly evident in Paul's theological understanding. ALL humanity fell into sin "in Adam," and conversely ALL humanity is redeemed and saved "in Christ" (cf. Romans 5:12-21). Jesus Christ represented us ALL in human and spiritual solidarity. Many find this difficult to fathom or comprehend, because this is so foreign to the Western mind and its individualistic orientation. From our individualism we struggle with the concept of being "in another," even choking on Paul's explanation that Levi was "in Abraham" making sacrifices before the High Priest, Melchizedek (Heb. 7:1-28).

When Jesus became the God-man in the incarnation He assumed identification as the "head" of the corporate life of the human race in its fallen and mortal condition (cf. Rom. 8:3). He was the corporate representation of humanity. One might even say that He was humanity representatively encompassed in One Person. Everything that happened to Him happened to us, because we were "in Him."

Earlier it was explained "ALL humanity is represented 'in Christ'," and "ALL humanity died when Christ died." The question was posed, "Where were you when Christ died?" You were there, for your were "in Christ." Where were you when Christ rose from the dead in the resurrection? You were there, for you were "in Christ." It is not a big step then to now advocate that ALL humanity is "*in Christ*," and "in **union** with Christ."

Yes, that solidarity wherein all mankind are connected and united "in Christ" means that there is an objective universal union of ALL men with Christ.

Previous mention was made of the objective universal of ALL humanity being graced by God "*in Christ Jesus*" (I Cor. 1:4), and "blessed with every spiritual blessing ... *in Christ*, and chosen *in Him* before the foundation of the world" (Eph. 1:3,4). "God has saved us and called us with a holy calling, not according to our works, but according to His own purpose and grace which was granted us *in Christ Jesus* from all eternity" (II Tim. 1:9,10). "Even when we were dead in our transgression, (God) made us alive together *with Christ*..., and raised us up *with Him*, and seated us *with Him* in the Heavenly places in Christ Jesus, so that in the ages to come He might show the surpassing riches of His grace in kindness toward us *in Christ Jesus*" (Eph. 2:5-7). There is ample biblical support to demonstrate the objective universal of ALL humanity being "*in Christ*." "By His doing you are *in Christ Jesus*, who became to us wisdom from God, and righteousness and sanctification, and redemption" (I Cor. 1:30).

• In continued expansion of this listing we could note that "ALL humanity is **sanctified** in Christ" and "ALL humanity is **glorified** in Christ" and "ALL humanity is **seated in the heavenlies** in Christ," but we will conclude this list (for the time being) by affirming that *ALL humanity is **drawn** to Christ by His Spirit.* In the final days before His crucifixion Jesus declared, "If I be lifted up (in crucifixion on a cross), I will draw ALL men to Myself" (John 12:32), and went on to explain to His disciples that He would send another (*allos* – of the same kind as Himself) Helper, the Holy Spirit, who would lead the disciples of Christ into all truth (cf. John 16:13), allowing them to see that ALL humanity is represented within the life, death and resurrection of Jesus Christ.

The self-giving nature of God desires, intends, and implements the drawing of ALL mankind into participation in the Trinitarian interpersonalism of His LOVE. Divine love, as exemplified in the perfect personal interaction of the Trinity, always reaches out to the "other," and the "other" extends to the "ALL men" of the divinely created human race.

I know that many Christians will have reservations about the foregoing list of the objective extent and efficacy of the life and work of Jesus Christ. Evangelical Christians, in particular, have tended to give more emphasis to the *subjective* response of human individuals rather than the *objective* action of God in Jesus Christ to which (and to Whom) they are responding. There are many, no doubt, who will question whether the scriptures cited in support of the above listed premises are legitimately interpreted. The same verses have often been interpreted both objectively and subjectively by various Christian persuasions for many centuries, and we must continue to allow for such dual interpretations without assuming that the one we are most familiar with is the only valid interpretation.

I suspect that if I were to conclude at this point, there would be some who have read the foregoing recitation of the objective-universal realities of God's work in the Son, Jesus Christ, who might be uncomfortable, if not downright agitated. They might have fears that this is a "universalist" teaching, or that I was certainly in danger of falling into such an heretical ditch. The more astute among you might be saying, "There's another side to the story. We want to hear the rest of the gospel." We shall proceed to consider the other side of the dialectic directly, but first let me drive home the objective-universal extent and efficacy of the Person and work of Jesus Christ.

What we are considering here it simply, and astoundingly, the "finished work" of Jesus Christ – the objective historical and theological work of Jesus Christ. From the cross Jesus exclaimed, "*Tetelestai*, It is finished!" (John 19:30). Jesus knew that He had done everything necessary to redeem humanity, to set in motion the restoration of the human race. He took the death consequences of humanity's sin, allowing the life of God (His own life) to be restored to human beings, so "man could be man as God intended man to be." His mission on earth was accomplished! *Fait accompli*! Signed, sealed, and delivered! There was nothing else that God could do, nor anything man could do, to accomplish, achieve, or add to the redemption and restoration of the human race. That is why Jesus tells the Father, "I have accomplished the work that You gave me to do" (Jn. 17: 4). This is the all-inclusive "finished work" of Jesus Christ. No one is left out (or "left behind" – to use a familiar lingo of another category of thought). Everyone is included – no human being is excluded from the grace of God in Jesus Christ! The age-old charge of Christian exclusivism is bogus and invalid – no one is excluded or "cut out" from the efficacy of what God has done for ALL mankind in the divine-human, God-man, Jesus Christ. The Christian gospel is not exclusive – It is inclusive! "God is not willing that any should perish" (II Peter 3:9). "Our life is hidden with Christ in God" (Col. 3:3). This objective-universal reality of Christ's life and work will eventually be acknowledged by ALL, when at the name of Jesus EVERY KNEE WILL BOW, of those who are in heaven and on earth and under the earth, and every tongue will confess that Jesus Christ is Lord, to the glory of God the Father" (Phil. 2:10,11).

There are some in the Christian community who want to dampen and tone down these objective-universal realities of Christ's work by saying that these are just "positional truths" that are merely posited to be true, but aren't really true until some additional action is taken, or until some future time. NO, these are not just posited positional truths, nor are they just juridical or forensic "declared truths" that have yet to be actuated. These are actual objective truths explaining the extent and efficacy of the life and work of Jesus Christ, and they are actually objectively effectual for ALL human persons – not just potentially effectual, but actually effectual objectively for every human individual that has lived, is living, and will ever live.

When I began this discussion of the objective-universal realities of Christ's work, I explained that these are enacted outside of us – objectively – by God. We have no part in enacting or effecting these realities of Christ. They are not contingent on our consent or cooperation. They are true whether we know about them or not, and whether we believe them or not. The Triune God took the Grace initiative to unilaterally implement and enact these spiritual realities with universal significance for ALL the world of mankind. These are the universal *indicatives* of God's action and revelation. All of the personal *imperatives* of response are on the side of the subjective-particular.

Recall the familiar phrase: "It's not what *we* do, but what *God* does!" Many times we have applied that to the subjective side of the equation, but it is just as valid here on the objective-universal side of the dialectic. The foundation of the gospel is grounded and constituted by what God has done in His Son Jesus Christ and by the power of His Holy Spirit. This – the objective-universal act of God in Jesus Christ is "good news" – it is phenomenal ... It is fantastic ... It is inclusive ... We are ALL included ... We have all been embraced by God's grace in Jesus Christ, and He won't let go! ... Do you find that to be as exciting as I do? ... Can you believe it? ... "Well ... yes, kind'a ... BUT ... (and as Dan Stone used to say, "It's what follows the 'but' that you really believe ... And it's what precedes the 'but' that one hesitantly believes, but not really ...).

When some Christians hear the recitation of the objective universal action of God in Christ, they conclude, "It's too good to be true!" And if they have been thoroughly "evangelicalized," these truths may seem so strange and foreign that they tragically react by hurling charges of heresy at the messenger of the gospel. ... "You've gone too far! ... off the edge ... You've become a liberal … a universalist!" … That just reveals how far Western Evangelical Christian teaching has over-emphasized the subjective-particular of what an individual is allegedly required to DO to be particularized as a "Christian," rather than emphasizing what God has DONE – objectively and universally accomplished in Jesus Christ. Much of Evangelicalism has slid off into the extremist ditch of "particularism" (and they do not even realize how "off-base" they are!).

My friends, these objective universal realities are so important that apart from realizing the amazing Grace of God on our behalf in Jesus Christ, objectively and universally, the only other conclusion one can draw is that mankind by his own action saves himself in the *autosoterion* of self-salvation – IMPOSSIBLE!

One more comment before we move on to the other side of the dialectic.

Question: Is it possible to push the emphasis on these objective-universal realities too far? Yes, without a doubt, it is possible! When they are not balanced with the subjective-particular truth-tenets of an individual's faith-response of receptivity to Jesus Christ, one can slide off into the extremist ditch of "universalism." But we must be careful not to "throw the baby out with the bathwater." I have attempted to list a number of objective-universal theses that seem to be defensible by legitimate biblical exegesis, though I am aware that not all will agree that the objective interpretations of the biblical texts utilized are legitimate. In due time we will come back to add a number of objective-universal assertions that seem to me to go beyond legitimate biblical documentation, and cause an over-emphasis on the objective-universal that the Christian community needs to beware of.

Subjective Particular

As we move on to the subjective-particular side of the dialectic of biblical assertions of the extent and efficacy of the Person and work of Jesus Christ, there will be many Christians who will find the assertions in this category to be just as problematic as other Christians find the assertions of the objective-universal to be problematic. Different theological streams of Christian thought have tended to emphasize one or the other, and to deemphasize the contrasting tenets.

The Protestant reformers, for example, were hesitant to venture or tread in the realm of the subjective-particular. Both Martin Luther and John Calvin tended to have an over-objectified emphasis on the Person and work of Christ that was leery of the subjective response and particular implications of the individual inwardness of the Christian faith, and that because medieval Roman Catholic theology had emphasized a subjective "infused grace" to enable Christians to do the righteous "works" God required of them. Luther emphasized the "alien righteousness" of

Christ, and was adamant that individual subjective response contributed nothing to what God accomplished in Jesus Christ. Calvin was even more dismissive of the subjective-particular, following Augustine's premise into the strange and amalgamated construct of "objective particularism" (as we will consider later) wherein the particulars of the extent and efficacy of Christ's work were objectively predetermined by God in electing some and not electing others. Both Luther and Calvin rejected their contemporary reformer, Andreas Osiander's emphasis on the subjective righteousness of Christ in the Christian. For those readers who have a Lutheran theological background, the objective-universal statements we have made probably do not sound strange at all. On the other hand, if you have a Reformed/Calvinistic/Presbyterian or Baptist theological background the objective-universal statements may sound quite foreign, because American evangelical thought has tended to have a Reformed perspective, but the subjective-particular elements that are to be considered directly may evoke uncomfortable reactions as well.

It needs to be noted here that there cannot be any subjective phenomena that particularizes individuals in relationship to God that has not been first freely extended to ALL persons in the objective-universal of God's activity. How can there be anything on the subjective side that hasn't first been offered and done on the objective side? The objective is foundational to the subjective. What has been accomplished by God *out*side of us (objectively), *for* us and *on our behalf*, can then consequently be experienced *in*side of us (subjectively). The subjective is but an individual human response to the objective reality of God's action. Only what has been extended by God's grace universally to ALL human beings can be responded to by individuals in order to make such experientially particular to themselves.

It will be instructive to commence by going back through the listing of objective-universal realities noted previously in order to explain that they usually have a correlation on the subjective-particular side of the dialectic. If there were not such opportunity, then there would be but a divine determinism whereby God implemented His will without any concern for human freedom of choice and consent, leading to some form of universalism. (*cf. Addendum G*)

- *All humanity is loved by God in Christ* (objective universal). We noted from John 3:16-18 that the subjective particular element is intermixed with the objective universal. "For God so loved the world that He gave His only begotten Son (objective universal), that whoever believes in (into) Him (subjective) shall not perish but have eternal life (the either-or particulars that result from the subjective response).

The objective love of God for the human race must be allowed to subjectively penetrate the inner man of an individual by means of faithful receptivity to facilitate an intimate, personal love relationship with God in Christ. Those who are not receptive to God's love in Christ are spiritually dead (I Jn. 3:14) and accursed (I Cor. 16:22), not knowing God (I Jn. 4:8) and not having the love of God in them (Jn. 5:42). Those who are open to God's love in Christ experience "the love of God poured out in their hearts through the Holy Spirit given to them" (Rom. 5:5) and enjoy a mutual internal abiding (cf. Jn. 17:23,26) relationship of love by the Spirit (I Jn.

4:13) because they are born of God and know God (I Jn. 4:7). Nothing external can separate them from the love of God in Christ (Rom. 8:35-39), but their love relationship will certainly be tested (Heb. 12:6; Rev. 3:19). In their Christian life they are continually "learning to live loved" and to draw ever closer to their Beloved, Jesus Christ.

• *All humanity has been graced by God in Christ* (objective universal). The objective and universal grace of God has appeared bringing salvation to ALL men (Titus 2:11), but God's grace action is applied individually when a particular human being is subjectively willing to become a "partaker of grace" (Phil. 1:7), receiving and nurturing "the grace of the Lord Jesus Christ in their spirit" (Philem. 1:25).

To the Roman Christians Paul explained, "it is by faith...in accordance with grace" (Rom. 4:16) that we partake of the promises of Abraham, and "obtain our introduction by faith into this grace in which we stand" (Rom. 5:2). "By grace you have been saved through faith" (Eph. 2:5,8), he advises the Ephesians.

The grace-dynamic of the living Lord Jesus becomes subjectively operative in the Christian (cf. II Cor. 9:15), who "draws near with confidence to the throne of grace" (Heb. 4:16), and continues to "grow in the grace and knowledge of their Lord and Savior Jesus Christ" (II Peter 3:18).

- *All humanity has been elected by God in Christ* (objective universal). God the Father, Son, and Holy Spirit has elected all men in the Chosen One, the Elect One, the God-man, Jesus Christ, making the choice to include the human race in the beneficial life and work of the Son.

Peter identified Jesus as the objective-universal "Elect Stone" (the cornerstone of redeemed humanity), but proceeded to write, "he who believes in Him (subjective particular) shall not be disappointed" (I Peter 2:6). Human individuals who identify with Jesus Christ become the particular "elect of God" when they "put on the new man" (Col. 3:12) and become "new creatures" (II Cor. 5:17). As "God's elect" (Rom. 8:33), God is always FOR them, not condemning them, but supplying them with everything necessary in the

Christian life by His grace as Jesus intercedes on their behalf. In the Revelation, John saw that those "who were with the Lamb (Jesus) are the called, chosen (elect) and faithful" (Rev. 17:14) – Christ-ones.

- *All humanity has been included in the death of Christ* (objective universal). Though Jesus Christ died a horrific death of crucifixion on the cross on behalf of ALL mankind, voluntarily willing to take the death consequences of sin on our behalf, and we were representatively included in His death, the dialectic demands a subjective and experiential realization of death within each individual spiritually.

Though objectively included in the historic death of Jesus, individual human beings retain the Adamic consequences of spiritual death, dead works, and physical mortality until such time as they are prepared by the Spirit to acknowledge, accept and appreciate the actualizing of Christ's life and work within their very being. "Dead in trespasses and sin" (Eph. 2:1,5) and identified with the death-dealer (Heb. 2:14; Eph. 2:2), the unregenerate individual consents to the death of their "old man" spiritual identity. "Buried with Him

(Jesus) through baptism into death" (Rom. 6:3,4), the believer is "united with Him in the likeness of His death" (Rom. 6:5) as the "old man is crucified with Him" (Rom. 6:6), whereby we "die to sin" (Rom. 6:2) and are "freed from sin" (Rom. 6:7) and its oppressive hold on our behavior. When the old spiritual identity has thus "died with Christ" (Rom. 6:8) and the individual has been "united with Christ in the likeness of His resurrection" (Rom. 6:5) with the spiritual identity of a "new man" (Eph. 4:24; Col. 3:10) in Christ, the new Christian has "passed out of death into life" (I Jn. 3:14) to "live with Him" (Rom. 6:8) and "walk in newness of life" (Rom. 6:4). "We have died and our life is hidden with Christ in God" (Col. 3:3). We can exclaim with Paul, "I have been crucified with Christ; and it is no longer I who live, but Christ lives in me; and the life which I now life in the flesh I live by faith in the Son of God, who loved me and gave Himself up for me" (Gal. 2:20).

You may have noticed that the same scripture citations that are utilized to explain the objective universal realities of our death with Christ are legitimately utilized to explain the subjective and particular experiencing of those realities. They have

59

been so utilized with such double entendre throughout the history of Christian interpretation.

- *All humanity has been forgiven in Christ* (objective universal). There can be no doubt that all forgiveness of sin must be the act of God for it is against Him and His character alone that sin is a violation and vile misrepresentation. The forgiveness of the sins of mankind is effected only in the redemption through the blood of Jesus Christ on the cross of Calvary (cf. Eph. 1:7).

In the quotation of Robert Capon cited previously he explains that the residents of both heaven and hell are all "forgiven sinners" (as ALL men are), but introduces the subjective particularizing of such by noting that those in heaven have *accepted* God's forgiveness in Christ and those in hell have *rejected* God's forgiveness in Christ.

The objective forgiveness is extended to all humanity universally, but the individual's internal and subjective experience of God's forgiveness is via the response of accepting and affirming God's action. When Peter proclaimed that the Jewish people had crucified the Messiah, they were "pierced in their heart, and cried out 'What shall we do?' Peter said to them, 'Repent, and each of you be baptized in the name of Jesus Christ for the *forgiveness* of your sins; and you will receive the gift of the Holy Spirit'" (Acts 2:38). Explaining his own call to ministry among the Gentiles, Paul was advised by the risen Christ to "turn" or convert them "from darkness to light, from the authority of Satan to God, that they may receive *forgiveness* of sins and an inheritance among those who have been sanctified *by faith* in Me'" (Acts 26:18).

• *All humanity has been reconciled to God in Christ* (objective universal). God took the initiative to alleviate any estrangement between Himself and humanity, who by their sin had created an enmity (Eph. 2:15) with God to the point of being "enemies" (Rom. 5:10). "God was in Christ reconciling the world to Himself (objective universal), not counting their trespasses against them" (II Cor. 5:19), Paul wrote to the Corinthians, but immediately following he pleads, "Therefore, ...we beg you on behalf of Christ, *be reconciled* to God" (II Cor. 5:20). In this personal imperative Paul turns to the subjective particular that necessitates an individual willingness to accept a reconciled relationship between parties that puts aside all previous differences and issues to allow for an *at-one-ment* of reconciliation and a union of interpersonal fellowship between God and a believer.

• *ALL humanity has been adopted as sons and daughters into the (objective-universal) family of God.* The family of humanity identified in disobedience has disintegrated in the obedience of Jesus Christ, and been adopted wholesale into the family of God.

The objective and universal adoption transfer of the human race can now be experienced in the subjective and particular realm of familial relationships. "Because you are sons," Paul advises the Galatians, "God has sent forth the Spirit of His Son into our hearts, crying 'Abba! Father!'" (Gal. 4:6). Herein we experience the spiritual intimacy of the Father-child relationship with God. "For all who are being led by the Spirit of God, these are sons of God. For you have not received a spirit of slavery leading to fear again, but you have received a spirit of *adoption* as sons by which we cry out, 'Abba! Father!'" (Romans 8:14,15).

Those who have "come out" from their identification with the spirit of error and affiliation with unbelievers are welcomed by the Lord saying, "I will be a father to you, and you shall be sons and daughter to Me" (II Cor. 6:15-18). "It is those who are of *faith* who are sons of Abraham" (Gal. 3:7), for we are "sons of God through *faith* in Christ Jesus" (Gal. 3:26). The human response of faith particularizes the subjective dynamics of the intimate interactions of our spiritual family.

Meanwhile, there remains a "not yet" expectation of the consummation of our adoption, for we are "waiting eagerly for our *adoption as sons*, the redemption of our body" (Rom. 8:23), and therein is our continuing hope in Christ Jesus.

• *All humanity has been saved in Christ* (objective universal). Humanity as a whole has been "made safe" from the consequences of sin in order to be restored to God's created functional intent for mankind. There is nothing any human being can do to effect or in any way amplify or even co-operate with God's saving action in the Savior, Jesus Christ. Salvation is a *fait accompli* for the entire human race.

The above assertion does not negate nor diminish the accompanying subjective involvement that particularizes the individual Christian's personal salvation. In the midst of one's human response, believing individuals are "made safe" from the enslavement of a spiritual condition of death and the dysfunction of sin in order to receive and function by means of the indwelling presence of the Spirit of Christ in the spirit of a receptive believer.

Whereas popular Christian thought has often succumbed to an event-centered idea of "getting saved" in an experience of conversion or regeneration, and the benefit of being able to point back to a particular date when an individual allegedly "got saved," the biblical usage of the term "salvation" is a much broader and more comprehensive soteriological term.

Reference to salvation or "being saved" is often connected in scripture with the subjective human response of faith: The Philippian jailer asked Paul and Silas, "Sirs, what must I do to be *saved*?" They said, "*Believe* in the Lord Jesus, and you will be *saved*, you and your household" (Acts 16:30,31). Paul explained to the Ephesians Christians, "For by grace you have been *saved* through *faith*; and that not of yourselves, it is the gift of God; not as a result of works, so that no one may boast" (Eph. 2:8,9). To the Romans he wrote, "This is the word of faith which we are preaching, that if you confess with your mouth Jesus *as* Lord, and *believe* in your heart that God raised Him from the dead, you will be *saved*; for with the heart a person believes, resulting in righteousness, and with the mouth he confesses, resulting in *salvation*" (Rom. 10:8-10). The Corinthians were instructed, "This is the gospel which I preached to you, which also you *received*, in which also you stand, by which also you are *saved*, if you hold fast the word which I preached to you, unless you *believed* in vain" (I Corinthians 15:1,2), for "God was well-pleased through the foolishness of the message preached to *save* those who *believe*" (I Cor. 1:21).

Salvation is not something that any individual possesses, nor is it anything that can be quantified in static objectified parameters. "Having been reconciled," Paul wrote, "you shall be *saved* by His life" (Rom. 5:10). By the dynamic functionality of the living Savior, Jesus

Christ, we subjectively allow Him to ontologically "work out our salvation" (Phil. 2:12) by His "saving life" expressed in our internal and external behavior. Only thus are we "protected by the power of God through faith for a salvation ready to be revealed in the last time" (I Pet. 1:5).

• *All humanity has been given God's life in Christ* (objective-universal). The death consequences of sin were taken by Jesus Christ in His death, and His subsequent resurrection from the dead brought life to the human race. Participation in the divine life of the Triune God, Father, Son, and Holy Spirit, is now the birthright of ALL humanity by the resurrection-birth (cf. Acts 13:33) of the divine-human and ever-living Jesus Christ.

On the subjective level of our particular experience, the residual effects of death remain in each human individual that is born. From natural birth each individual is "dead in trespasses and sins" (Eph. 2:1,5; Col. 2:13), "excluded from the life of God" (Eph. 4:18), "abiding in death" (I Jn. 3:14), and "devoid of the Spirit" (Jude 19). No one needs to remain in that condition, however, for God has done everything necessary and possible to extend and grant His life to ALL persons.

Not desiring that any should perish (II Pet. 3:9), God desires that each individual should exercise their God-given freedom of choice (subjective-particular) to receive the divine life that is already theirs (objective-universal) for the taking. "For God so loved the world that He gave His only begotten Son, that whoever believes into Him shall not perish, but have eternal life" (John 3:16).

The apostle John, above all the other biblical writers, explains the either-or particulars of our subjective human response to the divine life granted to us in Jesus Christ. "He who believes in the Son has eternal life; but he who does not obey the Son will not see life" (Jn. 3:36). "He who believes Him (God the Father) who sent Me (Jesus), has eternal life, and does not come into judgment, but has passed out of death into life" (Jn. 5:24; I Jn. 3:14). "He who has the Son has the life; he who does not have the Son of God does not have the life" (I Jn. 5:11,12). "These have been written so that you may believe that Jesus is the Christ, the Son of God; and that believing you may have life in His name" (Jn. 20:31).

Those who have "believed in Him (Jesus) for eternal life" (I Tim. 1:16), "we know that we have passed out of death into life" (I Jn. 3:14), delighting in the experiential reality that "Christ is our life" (Col. 3:4). Spiritual life, eternal life, divine life is not an entity or commodity detached from Jesus as a consequential benefit. No! Jesus is the very Being of the life of God (cf. Jn. 11:25; 14:6), and there is no life apart from His Being in action.

• *All humanity has been reckoned with God's righteousness in Christ* (objective universal). Because the unrighteousness of humanity has been "removed as far as the east is from the west" (Ps. 103:12) in the "righteous act" (Rom. 5:18) of the "Righteous One" (Acts 3:14; 7:52; 22:14), Jesus Christ, i.e. His death on the cross, the intrinsic righteousness of the character of God Himself has been applied to humanity at large.

The hallmark of the new covenant arrangement between God and humanity mediated by Jesus Christ (I Tim. 2:5) is that "the righteous shall live by faith" (Hab.

2:4; Rom. 1:17; Gal. 3:11; Heb. 10:38), not by the human performance efforts of attempting to keep the regulations of any law-based behavior. "The promise to Abraham and his descendants that he would be heir of the world was not through the Law, but through the righteousness of faith" (Rom. 4:13), "the righteousness of God through faith in Jesus Christ for all those who believe" (Rom. 3:22), "the righteousness which is by faith" (Rom. 9:30).

The particularity of participating in the righteous character of God experientially is via the resurrected life of the divine-human Person who embodies all divine Righteousness (I Cor. 1:30) causing the human spirit to be made alive by His righteousness (Rom. 8:10) as an individual exercises the subjective human response of faith. Paul's personal testimony was that he was "found in Him (Jesus), not having a *righteousness* of my own derived from the Law, but that which is through faith in Christ, the *righteousness* which *comes* from God on the basis of faith" (Phil. 3:9). To the Romans he wrote, "If you confess with your mouth Jesus as Lord, and believe in your heart that God raised Him from the dead, you will be saved; for with the heart a person believes, resulting in *righteousness*, and with the mouth he confesses, resulting in salvation" (Rom. 10:9,10).

The Christian believer has internally (subjectively) been "renewed in the spirit of the mind, and has put on the new self, which in the likeness of God has been created in righteousness and holiness of the truth" (Eph. 4:24). This spiritual identity of an indwelling "righteousness" is not inherent or intrinsic to the believer (only intrinsic to God), but is derived from the presence of the "Righteous One," the living Lord Jesus indwelling the human spirit. Such subjectively derived righteousness is explained within the new covenant scriptures as our being "made righteous" (Rom. 5:19) and "becoming the righteousness of God in Him (Jesus Christ)" (II Cor. 5:21). This important truth of the subjective-particular of a Christian's identity of righteousness was rejected by the reformers (both Luther and Calvin) in their repudiation of the theology of Andreas Osiander, in favor of the objectified and forensic assertion of "declared righteousness."

• *All humanity has been blessed in Christ* (objective universal). God promised Abraham that by his "seed,"

Jesus Christ (Gal. 3:16), "ALL nations would be blessed" (Gen. 12:3; Gal. 3:8). Indeed, ALL humanity from ALL nations has been *blessed* in the advent and passion of the God-man, Jesus Christ. "In Christ Jesus the blessing of Abraham has come to the Gentiles, so that we should receive the promise of the Spirit through faith" (Gal. 3:14). "Those who are of faith are blessed with Abraham, the believer" (Gal. 3:9).

The objective and universal blessing of God, wherein "He has blessed us with every spiritual blessing in heavenly places in Christ" (Eph. 1:3), becomes a particular subjective and internalized spiritual blessing when the individual responds to Jesus in the likeness of Abraham's faith and experientially participates in "every spiritual blessing in heavenly places."

Jesus pronounced His blessing upon those who follow Him in faith saying, "blessed are those who hear the word of God and observe it" (Lk. 11:28); "blessed is everyone who will eat bread in the kingdom of God" (Lk. 14:15); "blessed are those who do not see (visibly), and yet believe" (Jn. 20:29); "blessed are those who wash their robes, so that they may have the right to the tree of life, and may enter by the gates into the city" (Rev. 22:14).

Not all will appreciate our objective or subjective claims to God's blessing in Christ. The apostle Peter wrote, "If you are reviled for the name of Christ, you are *blessed*, because the Spirit of glory and of God rests on you" (I Pet. 4:14).

• *All humanity has been included "in Christ"* (objective universal). The divine-human God-man, Jesus Christ, inclusively represented ALL humanity in the entirety of His Being and activity. Every human person was "in Christ" when He "was made flesh" (Jn. 1:14) and "was made in the likeness of men" (Phil. 2:7), and when He died on the cross on every human person's behalf.

The objective-universal of *representative inclusion* "in Christ" is intended to allow for the subjective-particular of an individual's *relational inclusion* "in Christ." "If any man is *in Christ*, he is a new creature; old things have passed away, behold all things have been made new" (II Cor. 5:17). "By His doing you are *in Christ Jesus*, who became to us wisdom from God, and righteousness and sanctification, and redemption"

(I Cor. 1:30). Regardless of ethnicity, nationality, vocation, gender, "you are all one *in Christ Jesus*" (Gal. 3:28), states Paul.

When an individual believer receives the Spirit of Christ to dwell in their spirit (cf. Rom. 8:9,16), and becomes "alive to God *in Christ Jesus*" (Rom. 6:11), there is a double sense of internality: Christ is "in us" (cf. Gal. 2:20; Col. 1:27; II Cor. 13:5) and we are "in Christ." This subjective particularizing of our being "in Christ" involves an intimate personal relationship whereby we are personally included in all that He is – all that He is He is to me! Many Christians have found it helpful to read the subjective "in Christ" phrases within the New Testament with an implied meaning of "in union with Christ," thus personalizing their subjective spiritual oneness with the living Lord Jesus.

The phrase Paul uses in Romans 8:1, "There is now therefore no condemnation for those who are *in Christ Jesus*," can be interpreted objectively as noted previously, but can also be interpreted subjectively in the internal realization that there need be "no condemnation" of guilt within the conscience of those who have experienced complete forgiveness "in union with Christ."

• *All humanity has been drawn to Christ by the Spirit* (objective universal). God is relentless in His love to draw ALL men to Himself in Christ. "No one can come to Me," Jesus declared, "unless the Father who sent Me *draws* him; and I will raise him up on the last day" (Jn. 6:44). The poet, Francis Thompson, wrote a poem entitled *The Hound of Heaven* (1893), likening God's drawing and wooing of mankind to the relentless hunting hound chasing a hare, but God's grace does not seek to destroy us, but to redeem us.

The objective-universal of God's pursuit of grace must be juxtaposed with the subjective-particular of a human individual's willingness to be drawn into the intimacy of fellowship with God in Christ. "He (Jesus) is able to save forever those who *draw near* to God through Him, since He always lives to make intercession for them" (Heb. 7:25). "Let us *draw near* with confidence to the throne of grace, so that we may receive mercy and find grace to help in time of need" (Heb. 4:16). "Let us *draw near* with a sincere heart in full assurance of faith, having our hearts sprinkled clean from an evil conscience and our bodies washed with pure water" (Heb. 10:22). "*Draw near* to God and He will *draw near* to you" (James 4:8).

All of humanity, from "every tribe and language and people and nation" (Rev. 5:9;7:9), is drawn to Christ by the Spirit (objective-universal), but not all individuals will accept the wooing of the Spirit (subjective-particular). C. S. Lewis, in his marvelous book *The Great Divorce*, puts it this way: "There are two kinds of people in the end: those who say to God, 'Thy will be done,' and those to whom God says, in the end, '*Thy* will be done.'" God allows human beings to reject any subjective implications of what He has accomplished on our behalf in His Son, Jesus Christ.

Anthropological Understanding

Before we go any farther we must note that the subjective-particular of an individual's human response to what God has accomplished in Jesus Christ is predicated on a biblical recognition of how God created human beings – how the Creator God designed human creatures to function (*cf. Addendum H*). Apart from a biblically-based theological anthropology we cannot understand what the Creator God intended to transpire *inside* of the human individual – *subjectively*: We will either attribute *more* to the human individual than is valid – i.e. that human beings have a sovereign "free-will" that allows them to determine for themselves what they must do to implement their own salvation, **or** we will regard a human individual as having *less* ability to respond to God's action in Jesus Christ than is valid, implying that an individual human person is rendered sub-human and incapable of responding with "freedom of choice" to God's objective actions due to the consequences of sin that came upon humanity in the fall of Adam in the garden of Eden.

Unique among God's earthly creatures, human beings function at three levels: spiritually, psychologically and physiologically (cf. I Thess. 5:23). Contrary to the Greek dualist and binary concept of a human being a soul imprisoned in a body, the Christian perspective of human function recognizes the essential difference between spiritual function and psychological function (Heb. 4:12). That is why psychological remedies cannot resolve the spiritual needs of human beings. Personal human beings with spiritual function are capable of personal spiritual relationship with the personal divine Being of God Who is Spirit (cf. Jn. 4:24), and humans are capable of being indwelt by and united to the Spirit of God (cf. I Cor. 6:17) or Satan (cf. Eph. 2:3).

The tri-level function of created human beings is unlike the function of the Triune Creator God. Whereas God exists singularly *a se*, in Himself, and functions *ek autos*, out of Himself, autonomously and independently expressing His own intrinsic Being in His activity of grace – created human beings are derivative creatures having extrinsic being derived from beyond themselves, functioning only dependently and contingently by deriving from a spirit-source, which was intended to be the indwelling source of the Triune God – Father, Son and Holy Spirit. Unable to be an "independent self," the human being must derive spiritual identity, nature, character, image and destiny from a spirit-source, either God (*ek Theos*) or Satan (*ek diabolos*). A human being is a derivative creature.

Human derivation is not, however, determined by a forced or imposed spiritual operative or force – either divine determinism or diabolic determinism. The Creator God desired a freely chosen interpersonal relationship with human creatures, and Self-limited His Almighty omnipotence (as only God Himself could do), allowing created human beings the freedom of choice to receive from a spirit-source, and to derive character from God or Satan. This "freedom of choice" is not equivalent to "free-will," for the Creator God alone has the Free-will to Self-determine His action in accord with His intrinsic character, and then to Self-implement such Self-determined action out of His own inherent and independent divine power. Thus defined, the prerogative of Free-will can be attributed to God alone. As part of their *essentia humanum* human beings have been given "freedom of choice" to select the derivational source and supply of their spiritual, psychological and physiological function. This instrumentality of human "freedom of choice" allows humanity to exercise their human agency of "response-ability" to respond to God's action of grace to redeem and restore humanity in Jesus Christ, and to accept or reject a personal relationship with the Triune God. Human beings, even in their fallen spiritual condition of sinfulness, are volitionally self-determinative creatures who by their essential "freedom of choice" can respond to God (or to the Satanic alternative) with definite teleological consequences, one way or the other.

The subjective-particular side of the dialectic we are looking at is predicated on an anthropological understanding of God's having created human beings as "derivative creatures" – dependent, contingent, faith-creatures. Even in a sinful spiritual condition of unregeneracy a human individual is not essentially evil, nor has that person forfeited the basic human ability to respond to God in a divinely constituted and contextualized human freedom (cf. Augustinian/ Calvinism). Nor is the fallen human individual a sovereign, independent-self who by an alleged free-will can self-initiate a relationship with God, or do whatever might be deemed necessary to co-operate with God to effect a proper relationship between them.

(cf. *Addenda S* for a graphic chart concerning theological anthropology.)

Human Response has no Merit

We must be careful to note that in the subjective-particularization of human response to what God has done objectively and universally in Jesus Christ, our human response must not be construed to have any merit or any sense of accomplishment in restoring humans to a right relationship with God. Only GOD can effect the salvation humanity needs and requires by their collective rejection of God via Adam in the fall. And He, God, has done everything necessary to restore ALL human beings into a participatory relationship with the Triune Persons of the Godhead – Father, Son, and Holy Spirit. There is nothing more that needs doing; there is nothing more that any human being can DO to save himself from the consequences of the fall of the human race into sin and death. Human response does NOT effect the redemption or regeneration necessitated within a human individual. Human response is merely the receptivity to allowing God's action to be subjectively particularized and implemented in an individual's inner being.

We must ever remember that the "finished work" of Jesus Christ is FINISHED! All that needs doing is done! Humanity has been given the complete and perfect finished work of Christ for salvation and the restoration of God's life. No human effort is required or allowed!

In the objective-universal categories of the gospel we recognize that Christ died for ALL human beings. In the subjective-particular category we recognize that Christ died for ME ... yes, for ME, ... even ME ... the "least of all" (cf. Eph. 3:8) as Paul claimed, ... "to one untimely born" (I Cor. 15:8). Remember: In the area of the subjective-particular, we cannot experience individually anything that the objective-universal of God's activity has not previously *effected* for ALL men in Jesus Christ. The objective pardon allows for the subjective participation. The objective inclusion allows for the subjective impartation of the very life of the living Lord Jesus Christ.

Some Christian teachers and writers have referred to "God's part" and "man's part" in salvation. They do a great disservice to the understanding of the gospel. There is no "man's part" – this is not a cooperative endeavor. Salvation is God's endeavor – and God's endeavor alone! There is nothing that human beings can do to add to, to augment, to enhance, or to further advance the work of God in redeeming and restoring humanity in the God-man, Jesus Christ. We cannot save ourselves! There is no such thing as *autosoteria* – i.e. self-salvation by our own performance or works! We do not want to imply or give any impression that man's response DOES anything to contribute, merit, or take credit for an individual's salvation. The subjective-particularizing of human response is not meritorious or creditable. In the human response to the work of Jesus Christ there is nothing to commend the responder for so doing. It might be said, "FAITH is not commendable!" There is nothing for which the responder is worthy of praise, admiration, honor, acclaim, or for which the respondent is worthy of being extolled, lauded, or deserving of acknowledgment. Not even an "atta-boy" or "atta-girl" should be credited to the one who responds to Jesus –just an inner rejoicing for that person's having availed themselves to the eternal and inexpressible beauty of the life of God in Christ, in order to be "man as God intended man to be."

However we might be, or by whatever means by which we might have been, impacted by what God has done in Christ for ALL mankind, our response is simply, "Oh, I see! … Yes, Lord! … Thank you Lord! …"count me IN!" It is an affirmation of appreciation for God's promised action in Jesus Christ (cf. II Cor. 1:20). Our response is just the "AMEN" to God's action. "Yes, Lord, … so be it … let it be … verily, verily!" … even in ME! When we realize what God has done for us in Christ, we are open and available to the actualizing and personalizing of the objective divine realities in our personal lives and experience. No human performance is required or allowed – we just acknowledge, accept, agree, avail ourselves of what God has provided in Jesus Christ, and appreciate the experiential actualizing and authentication of God's work within us. There is no sense of achievement or accomplishment in this receptivity of the person and work of Jesus Christ.

The subjective response of a human individual that particularizes the work of Jesus Christ as effective IN that receptive person is perhaps best expressed as "thanksgiving." "Thank you, Lord, for doing this FOR me and IN me." The Greek word for "thanksgiving" is the word from which we get "Eucharist." It is the compound of two Greek words, *eu* meaning "good," and *charis* meaning "grace." In thanksgiving we simply express our awareness and acknowledgment of the "good grace" of God in Jesus Christ. The entire Christian life becomes the gratitude of a *eucharistic* appreciation of worship and prayer – of faith and obedience – and that is why many Christian groups stress the meaning of the Eucharist, with many brethren engaging in this remembrance every week – an ongoing human response of thanksgiving for Jesus Christ.

Christians should avoid all human attempts to calculate or quantify the response of an individual in human measurements. "How sorry or repentant are you? How firmly do you believe? How thankful are you? Does this individual have enough faith? How committed, dedicated or consecrated is this person? How sure are you that Jesus has come to live in you?" The subjective response of an individual should <u>not</u> be qualified or quantified with these kinds of human prescriptions, for this tends to give our human responses a measurable substantiation that ever so subtly gives weight to our human action. Every person must be allowed to respond and interact with the living Lord and Savior in his/her own personal way. Personal relationships commence uniquely in every case – there is no formulized procedure for entering into a relationship – and that includes the relationship of an individual with Jesus Christ.

The Human Response of Faith

Human response to God's redemptive and restorative action in Jesus Christ is broadly identified through the new covenant literature as "faith." In approximately two hundred texts throughout the New Testament "faith" is explained to be the condition of human response to the work of Christ. Though some would say that God's salvific work in Jesus Christ is unconditioned by any response of human individuals, the New Testament evidence seems to conclusively indicate the conditioned necessity of an individual human response of faith. The saving work of God in Christ is conditioned on the subjective-particular side of the dialectic by an individual's faith-response, and by such a response of acceptance and identification with

Jesus Christ an individual is particularized as a Christ-one, a Christian. Not every person will make such a faith-response to Jesus Christ. Not everyone in the world will be interested in being saved subjectively and experientially. This is the "not all" side of the dialectic.

The Philippian jailer asked, "What must I do to be saved?" Paul and Silas answered, "*Believe* in the Lord Jesus Christ and you will be saved..." (Acts 16:30,31). The apostle John explained, "As many as *received* Him, to them He gave the right to become children of God, *even* to those who *believe* in His name..." (John 1:12,13). The crowds of people in Galilee asked Jesus, "What must we do to work the works of God?" and Jesus responded. "This is the work of God (what God desires), that *you believe* in him (Me) whom He (God the Father) has sent" (Jn. 6:28,29). The Greek noun translated "faith" and "belief" in the New Testament is the same Greek word, *pistis*; the Greek verb *pisteuo* is translated into English as "to believe," but we do not have an English verb "to faith" – we do not refer to "faithing." So what does the human response of faith or believing entail?

It is most regrettable that so much of the Christian world has explained that the subjective response of the human individual to God's action in Jesus Christ is merely a cognitive, rational affirmation and assent to objective truth-tenets, indicating that acceptance of Jesus is by mental assent to propositional assertions. This has had tragic results for the Christian faith as a whole, casting it as a belief-system rather than the receipt of the living Lord Jesus. Our response of faith is not just a cerebral procedure, a "head-trip" of assent, but is rather an opening up of ourselves, our entire being, spirit, soul and body, in thankful receptivity to the presence and activity of the living Lord Jesus.

Faith is not just mental assent. Neither is faith just an internal, subjective emotional euphoria. Faith is not an ambiguous mystical state of being that is beyond description or definition. To put it as simply as it can be stated, "Faith is a choice!" – and human beings are choosing creatures. Faith is the human action of choosing. A longer definition might be: "Faith is a self-determined human volitional action utilizing our God-given human freedom of choice to respond in receptivity to what God has accomplished *for* us in Jesus Christ, and to what God desires to do *in* us, both initially and continually." Faith is a choice that human beings can make in their will. "Whosoever *will*, let him take of the water of life freely" (Rev. 22:17). On the other hand, Jesus indicted some religious leaders, saying, "You are un*willing* to come to Me, so that you may have life" (Jn. 5:40).

In the explanation, "faith is a human action of choice in the will," how do we avoid the charge that some make that such a human act of faith is a "work"? The apostle Paul is very clear in his statement to the Ephesians that "for by grace are we saved by faith, ... *not of works*, so that no man should boast" (Eph. 2:8.9). Though faith is a human action, we must not get snared in the logical fallacy that every action is a "work." Every "work" is an action, but every action is not a "work." A "work" implies performance, effort and accomplishment that has merit, or credit, or compensation. The human act of faith is not a "work" in that sense.

Consider this illustration. Suppose someone anonymously sends you a check made out in your name for $10,000. The money is yours if you want it. But when you get to the bank, they are going to ask you **do** something – the human action of signing your name and endorsing the check. Is the signing of your name a "work," a human action that could in any way be construed to indicate that by your performance you had earned the $10,000? Of course not! The $10,000 was simply a gift, and inscribing your signature was the only way to receive it. In like manner, the human action of faith is the only way to receive God's gift of Jesus Christ, and such faith cannot be misconstrued to be a "work" of performance or self-effort by which you merited or earned the gift.

Paul explained to the Romans that we are "justified as a *gift* by His *grace* through the redemption which is in Christ Jesus" (Rom. 3:24), and this becomes personally effective for "the one who has *faith* in Jesus" (Rom. 3:26). The human response of faith does not in any way create a legal obligation that requires God to act because of our human act. It does not create a contingency that coerces God into further action. God has already acted decisively by His grace to objectively, unilaterally and universally justify all sinful human beings by the free act of the Son, Jesus Christ, to take the sins of all mankind upon Himself, and the personal effects of such are made available to us by the human response of faith. Faith is not a "work" of human effort –

and to assert such is to misunderstand and deny God's Grace action in Jesus Christ.

The question might be asked, "What does faith DO?" Does the human action of a faith-choice accomplish or effect anything? In stating above that faith is not a work involving performance, effort or accomplishment we have answered the foregoing question in the negative. Human faith does not DO anything! Someone might counter, "But doesn't faith move mountains?" No, faith is just the choice of a personal willingness to watch God move mountains – as only God can do!

British Bible teacher, W. Ian Thomas, illustrated human faith in likeness to the clutch mechanism of a manual transmission automobile. The clutch is not the power source that provides locomotion to the automobile – that would be the engine. The clutch (which requires an action on the part of the human driver) is the mechanism that allows the power of the engine to be transferred to the drive train that causes the wheels to turn. In like manner our human faith allows the power of God in the action of the Son, Jesus Christ, to apply the redemptive work of the Savior to our personal life, and to continue to allow the life of Christ by the Spirit to function in the behavior of our Christian life.

Having noted that human faith is not to be regarded as a "work" of human effort, it is equally important to explain that human faith is not the gift of God. Yes, many well-meaning Christian teachers have made this assertion that "faith is the gift of God," but this is a misguided and dangerous teaching. Without a doubt, God's creation of the human race graciously provided mankind with the freedom of choice wherewith to make the choices of faith, but to indicate that God makes the faith-choice in us or deterministically causes us to make a faith-choice renders the freely chosen faith-love relationship between God and man meaningless. Faith is not the gift of God; it is a human response-ability.

The assertion that "faith is the gift of God" began centuries ago in the thought of Augustine (A.D. 354-430) whose anthropological understanding denied the human response of faith as explained above. In his book *On the Predestination of the Saints* (chapter 16), he writes, "Faith ... is God's gift. ... this gift is given to some, while to some it is not given." Twentieth century author, A.W. Pink concurred in his book *The Sovereignty of God* (pg. 101), writing, "Faith is God's gift, and the purpose to give it only to some, involves the purpose not to give it to others. ... "if there are some to whom He (God) purposes not to give faith, it must be because He ordained that they should be damned."

The Augustinian/Calvinist perspectives of both God and man do not seem to correlate with the biblical revelation. How could a loving God arbitrarily and capriciously elect some for salvation and not others? How could the God who sent His own Son to die for the sins of mankind disallow the efficacy of such redemption for a segment of humanity? How could a just God grant faith to some and withhold faith from other persons, and then judge the latter for unbelief, purposing that they should be damned? IF "faith is the gift of God," then I should think that the all-encompassing Love of God would cause ALL men to believe, and God could not blame anyone for their unbelief. Yes, there are some who would affirm such a universalistic thesis, but it does not seem to be the teaching of the scripture.

The words of W. Ian Thomas are very perceptive:

"Some would have you believe that only those can obey the Gospel and accept Christ as their Saviour, to whom God has given the ability to obey as a purely arbitrary, mechanical act on His part, leaving no option in the matter to any individual either way! ... such an idea can only serve to bring the righteousness and judgment of God into contempt and disrepute. It is your inherent right to choose which is at the very heart of the mystery, both of the mystery of godliness and of the mystery of iniquity." (*The Mystery of Godliness* – pg. 128)

"Never allow anyone to deceive you into believing that God has placed an arbitrary limitation upon the efficacy of the blood of Christ, or that there are those who cannot repent, even if they would, simply because God has deliberately placed them outside the scope of His redemptive purpose! This blasphemes the grace, the love and the integrity of God, and makes Him morally responsible for the unbelief of the unbeliever, for the impenitence of the impenitent, and saddles Him squarely with the guilt of the guilty – as an aider and abettor of their sin! Such is not the teaching of the Bible, for the Lord Jesus Christ made it abundantly clear that the reluctance is on man's part, not on God's! (*The Mystery of Godliness* – pg. 127)

To be fair, we must note that there are some within the Augustinian/Calvinist tradition who have denied that faith is God's gifted action. Writing in *The Dictionary of New Testament Theology* (article on "faith"), R. Bultmann states, "unlike Augustine, Paul never describes faith as a gift of God." Thoroughly Calvinistic author, John Murray, in his book *Redemption – Accomplished and Applied* (pg. 106) writes, "Faith is not the act of God. Faith is a response on the part of the person and of him alone." G.C. Berkouwer, in his book *Faith and Justification* (pg. 179) explains that "to ascribe faith to the grace of God is to invite subtle heresy."

There are two texts in particular that are popularly utilized by those who allege that faith is not a freely chosen human response to what God has done (and is doing) in Jesus Christ, but that faith is elicited and enacted by God and implemented by Jesus Christ on our behalf. The first passage thus interpreted is Ephesians 2:8,9 where Paul writes, "For by grace you have been saved through faith; and that not of yourselves, *it is* the gift of God..." This verse does not indicate that "faith" is "not of yourselves, but the gift of God," rather the reference is to the verb action of salvation; i.e. salvation is not of yourselves, it is the gift of God. Proper exegetical techniques must be utilized to interpret the text. The second verse often utilized to justify that faith is not a human response is Galatians

2:20, "I have been crucified with Christ; and it is no longer I who live, but Christ lives in me; and the *life* which I now live in the flesh I live by *faith in the Son of God*..." The King James Bible translates the last phrase, "I live by the *faith of the Son of God*...", utilizing a subjective genitive interpretation rather than an objective genitive interpretation (as the majority of later translations employ). Most Greek scholars and theologians agree that the "faith" referred to is the Christian's human response, and that the object of such faith is the Son of God, Jesus Christ. (cf. Rom. 3:22; Gal. 2:16)

Continuing our discussion of the "human response of faith," we should note that William Barclay (*The Mind of Saint Paul*, pg 112) wrote, "the first element in faith is what we can only call *receptivity* ... not receptivity of facts or the significance of the facts, ... but the receptivity of the person of Jesus Christ." James Moffatt likewise explains (*Grace in the New Testament*, pg. 132) faith as "the attitude of *receptivity* towards the gift of God." J. Gresham Machen in his classic book, *What is Faith?* (pg. 195) states, "The gift of God is eternal life through Jesus Christ our Lord. The *reception* of that gift is faith; faith means not doing something, but *receiving* something; it means not the earning of a reward but the acceptance of a gift." These comments are in accord with the New Testament record. "As many as *received* Him, to them He gave the right to become children of God, *even* to those who *believe* in His name" (John 1:12), states John. Paul asks the Galatians, "Did you *receive* the Spirit by the works of the Law, or by hearing with *faith?*" (Gal. 3:2), expecting his readers to respond that they received the Spirit by faith. Admonishing the Colossians, Paul writes, "As you *received* Christ Jesus the Lord, so walk in Him ... established in your *faith*" (Col. 2:6,7). Believing is receiving! Faith is our human receptivity of the divine activity of God in Christ. Such a definition disallows any charge of human passivism, for inherent in the definition is the necessary consequent of God's grace activity. This correlates with James' dictate, "Faith without works (without the consequential outworking of God's action) is useless;" it is "dead" (James 2:17,20,26). Faith is not faith if it is not receiving from God and allowing for the outworking of behavioral expression of God's character in Christian living.

Either/Or Particularization

We return to the subject at hand in the second thesis of the dialectic – the realization that the subjective-particular consideration of the extent and efficacy of the life and work of Jesus Christ implies that **NOT ALL** human individuals will respond to Jesus Christ in faith; **NOT ALL** people desire or will decide to avail themselves of life in Christ; **NOT ALL** will choose to receive the salvation available in the singular Savior of mankind; **NOT ALL** are interested in a spiritual exchange by which they can be re-lifed in regeneration at the core of their being; **NOT ALL** are concerned about an eternal destiny in the heavenly presence of God.

Despite what God has objectively and universally accomplished for ALL men by His grace (cf. Jn. 1:17) in the "finished work" of Jesus Christ, the subjective particularization implemented by our human "freedom of choice" produces the either-or categories that reveal that **NOT ALL** want to take advantage of what God has done on our behalf in His Son Jesus Christ. This inner, subjective, freedom of choice that God has given to all human persons in creation allows individuals to respond to God's objective grace-action in Jesus Christ by either receiving or rejecting what God has accomplished for ALL mankind. By such a choice of acceptance or rejection individuals are particularized as either Christ-ones, Christians, or as those who have opted out of Christ's salvation in the rejection of unbelief.

This accounts for the explicit either-or contrasts that are drawn in the new covenant scriptures. Paul contrasts the spiritual identities of the unregenerate "*old man*" with those who have "put on the *new man*" in regeneration (Eph. 4:22-24; Col. 3:9,10). Writing to the Corinthians, he differentiates between the "*natural man* who does not accept the things of the Spirit of God" and a "*spiritual man*" (I Cor. 2:14; 3:1), so designated because the Spirit of God dwells in that person. Prior to their becoming Christians the Ephesians were "*sons of disobedience*" (Eph. 2:2), but to the Galatian Christians Paul explains that they "are *sons of God* through faith in Christ Jesus" (Gal. 3:26), and John explains that the contrast is obvious – "the children of God and the children of the devil are obvious" (I John 3:10). "While we were yet *sinners*, Christ died for us" (Rom. 5:8), but we have been made "*saints*" (Eph. 1:18) by the presence of Jesus Christ, the Holy One, becoming the basis of who we are. There are those who are spiritually "*dead* in trespasses and sins" (Eph. 2:1,5), contrasted with those who "have passed out of death into *life*" (I John 3:14), for "he who has the Son has the life, and he who does not have the Son of God does not have the life" (I Jn. 5:12). Though we once belonged to the community of the "*world*" (cf. I Pet. 5:9; I Jn. 4:5), Christians are "not of the world" (Jn. 17:10), having been delivered from the domain of darkness, and transferred to the *kingdom* of His beloved Son" (Col. 1:13), whose "kingdom is not of this world" (Jn. 18:36). Whereas our spiritual source was once "the spirit that works in the sons of disobedience" (Eph. 2:2) and without the "Spirit of Christ" we could not be considered Christians (Rom. 8:9), Christians have been converted from "the dominion of *Satan to God*" (Acts 26:18), a radical dichotomy of derived spiritual being. The either-or contrast of designation and destiny is apparent in Matthew 25 where Jesus explains that "all the nations will be gathered before Him; and He (the Son of God) will separate them from one another, as the shepherd separates the *sheep* from the *goats*" (25:32), and "these (the unrighteous) will go away into eternal punishment, but the righteous into eternal life" (25:46).

The either-or contrasts that are the consequence of human subjective-particularization in individual "freedom of choice" cannot be overlooked or denied. **NOT ALL** utilize their response-ability of choice to receive in faith what God has objectively accomplished for them in Jesus Christ.

It must be admitted that many of the scripture texts just cited can be, and have been, interpreted from both an objective and subjective perspective. Those emphasizing the objective-universal work of Christ may use these verses as documentation of that thesis, and those emphasizing the subjective-particular response to the work of Christ may use these verses, as we have just done, to document this facet of the gospel. Such variances of interpretation have existed for centuries in Christian thought, and we must continue to allow for such.

We noted earlier that subjective human response is not merely mental assent to objective data. Faith is more than just receptivity to the historical details of redemption and the theological explanations of how the historical Jesus facilitates the possibility of humanity becoming the recipients of His eternal life. The "Christ of history" (objectively enacted) is the "Christ of experience" (subjectively encountered). The gospel of Jesus does not end at the incarnation, or the cross, or the resurrection, or Pentecost, or with the history of the early church. Nor can it be encapsulated in the theological formulations that have become the tradition of the church. Paul asked the Corinthians, "Do you not realize that Jesus Christ is IN you, unless you fail the test" of faith (II Cor. 13:5). If Christians are not cognizant that the risen and living Lord Jesus has come by His Spirit to live in them, to be their life, then the gospel is short-circuited and becomes a "dead-end story" – just another history lesson or theological discussion. In fact, Paul seems to be saying that to be unaware that the living Christ has come to indwell an individual is indicative of a failure in the exercise of faith that receives His presence into that person. When a person receives Christ Himself, they will undoubtedly be aware of His indwelling presence.

The subjective-particularization of human response to Jesus Christ must be inclusive of the indwelling presence and function of the entirety of the divine presence of Father, Son, and Holy Spirit. The faith-receptivity by which we particularize ourselves in identification and union with the living Christ involves the reception of the entire Trinity into our inner being. We become "partakers of the divine nature" (II Pet. 1:4). God the Father dwells in the Christian (Jn. 14:17,23; I Jn. 4:12,15,16). God the Son dwells in the Christian (Jn. 14:20; Rom. 8:10; Eph. 3:17; Heb. 3:14). God the Spirit dwells in the Christian (Rom. 8:9-11; Gal. 4:6). This reception of the divine presence of God into the spirit of an open and available individual occurs as the individual is "born of the Spirit" (John 3:5,6) in regeneration.

The presence and work of the Spirit of the Triune God is a primary indication of the extent and efficacy of the life and work of Jesus Christ as it is subjectively particularized in a receptive individual. Undue emphasis on the objective work of God in Christ usually diminishes or ignores the reality of the indwelling function of the divine Spirit. This is the reason why awareness of pneumatological realities is sadly lacking in those who over-emphasize the objective factors of the gospel to the neglect of the subjective, internal experience of the three-in-one divine Spirit. The "*Spirit of God* dwells in you" (I Cor. 3:6), Paul advises the Corinthians. If "anyone does not have the *Spirit of Christ*, he is none of His" (Romans 8:9-11), he writes to the Romans. "The Holy Spirit dwells in you" (II Tim. 1:14), is his reminder to Timothy. The Christian is one who has *received* the Holy Spirit (Acts 19:2), been *baptized* in the Spirit (I Cor. 12:13), and continues to be *filled* with the Spirit (Eph. 5:18) and to *walk* in the Spirit (Gal. 5:16). This internal spiritual indwelling of the divine Spirit (cf. I Cor. 3:16; II Tim. 1:14) is integral to the subjective particularity of the personal appropriation of the gospel. So much so that Paul explains that apart from the presence of the ontological essence and expression of the living Christ by His Spirit, one cannot be considered a Christian (cf. Rom. 8:9). Hear the words of C.S. Lewis,

> "When Christians say the Christ-life is in them, they do not mean simply something mental or moral. When they speak of being 'in Christ' or of Christ being 'in them,' this is not simply a way of saying that they are thinking about Christ or copying Him. They mean that Christ is actually operating through them..." (*Mere Christianity*. Pg. 64).

> (the) Christian idea of 'putting on Christ'... It is the whole of Christianity. Christianity offers nothing else at all. It differs from ordinary ideas of 'morality' and 'being good.'" (*Mere Christianity*, pg. 166)

The indwelling presence and function of God the Father, the living Christ, and the empowering Spirit changes the individual from the inside out. This is not a change in our humanness, our *essentia humanum.* It is not a change in anthropological ontology, for our humanity still functions as God created it to function, but this is an ontological change of "being" in our spirits. A spiritual exchange occurs within when the spirit of the world is exchanged for the Spirit of God (I Cor. 2:12), when the spirit of slavery is exchanged for the spirit of adoption (Rom. 8:15, when the spirit of error is exchanged for the spirit of truth (I Jn. 4:6), when the "spirit that works in the sons of disobedience" (Eph. 2:2) is exchanged for the Spirit of Jesus Christ (Phil. 1:19). An ontological exchange within our spirit precipitates a change in our derived identity and "being" from one spirit to another. This is the ontological reality that occurs in conversion and regeneration when we "turn from darkness to light and from the dominion of Satan to God" (Acts 26:18). The Christian becomes a "new creature in Christ" (II Cor. 5:17). Such is the basis for Paul's statement, "It is no longer I who live, but Christ lives in me" (Gal. 2:20). Herein we observe another of the either-or particularities whereby we have "put off the old man" and "put on the new man" (Eph. 4:22-24; Col. 3:9,10) in terms of subjective experience.

Let us be clear though that the indwelling divine presence is not just a punctiliar event or experience whereby the Spirit of Christ is placed within a location in the human spirit as a deposit for future benefits. "God has sent forth the Spirit of His Son into our hearts" (Gal. 4:6) that "Christ might be formed in us" (Gal. 4:19) – that the reality of His life and character might be "manifested in our mortal flesh" (II Cor. 4:11). "Having been reconciled (objectively), we shall be saved by His life (subjectively)" (Rom. 5:10), Paul explained to the Roman Christians. We participate in the "saving life of Christ" (cf. W. Ian Thomas) as the living Lord Jesus becomes the ontological dynamic of what we call "the Christian life." In the words of Thomas Merton, "Jesus creates it (the Christian life) in our souls by the action of His Spirit" (*The New Man*. Pg. 165). That is why Jesus told His disciples, "Apart from Me, you can do nothing" (Jn. 15:5) – nothing that expresses godliness or the intent and character of God. Only Christ can live the Christ-life – the Christian life! Christianity IS Christ! It is an abomination that naturalized Christian religion constantly attempts to detach and sever Christianity from the divine presence and divine dynamic of the living Lord Jesus. Christian living must be viewed as the very Being of God in Christ by the Spirit functioning and operating in a Christian's life – the very Being and doing of the living Lord Jesus. "We are His workmanship, created in Christ Jesus for good works, which He has prepared beforehand that we should walk in them" (Eph. 2:10). "Now may the God of peace ... equip you in every good thing to do His will, *working in us* that which is pleasing in His sight, *through* Jesus Christ, to whom be the glory forever and ever" (Heb. 13:20,21). The entirety of Christian living is the outworking of Christ's activity as the Christian continues to walk in faith, the continued receptivity of His (Christ's) activity. "As you received Christ Jesus, so walk in Him" (Col. 2:6) – by faith.

Personal Testimony

The subjective-particular of experiential participation in the indwelling presence and expression of the Christ-life has been the focus and emphasis of my involvement in Christian ministry for the past four decades (since 1973). Ministering in locations around the world, I have shared the good news of the indwelling risen Lord Jesus and the spiritual union created when the Spirit of Christ occupies a receptive individual's spirit.

This study on the "extent and efficacy of the life and work of Jesus Christ" presents a much larger perspective of Christian thought, but provides no contradictions whatsoever with what I have taught previously. It is but an attempt to see the "big picture" of the objective and subjective, the universal and the particular, elements of the gospel. In so doing I have no desire or intent to diminish the focus of ministry that God has called me to. I am convinced that the message of "Christ in you, the hope of glory" (Col. 1:27) is the essential core-reality of the Christian faith that Christians need to hear and experience today, and that is why I founded Christ in You Ministries and the christinyou.net website in the 1990s.

The subjective inwardness of the presence and function of Christ's life in the Christian is a crucial emphasis for contemporary Christians and the church in our day. In the Reformation, Martin Luther emphasized the *objective*-universal of God's work in Christ, while John Calvin emphasized the *objective*-particular of God's predetermined selection of the "elect" and the "non-elect." Both of the two foremost Protestant reformers gave lip-service to the concept of *sola fide*, "faith alone" as the response to the gospel, but Protestantism as a whole has suffered from an over-objectified focus on the divine action effected *outside* of the Christian individual, with little or no explanation of what God intends to transpire *inside* of the Christian. Without the inner experiential awareness of the Spirit of Christ in the spirit of an individual (cf. Rom. 8:9,16), Christian faith is reduced to mental assent to historical and theological data – nothing more than a belief-system with accompanying moral obligations.

I am not the only one to have made this observation. Twentieth century Anglican theologian, E. L. Mascall records a remark that "the great systems of Protestant dogmatics are magnificently articulated, tremendously imposing, and – because they fail to allow for any point of contact between God and man – entirely unusable." (86). Emil Brunner, the 20th century Swiss theologian, wrote:

> "Post-Reformation theology indeed denied the presence of the human partner, in order to prevent any possibility of man having any share of merit or any reason for self-congratulation, boasting, and it believed that it was necessary to surrender the role of the human subject as itself present, and to reduce it to the pure passivity of an object. But in doing so it completely destroyed the Pauline conception." (*Dogmatics III.* pgs 279,280)

Contemporary Anglican theologian, Alister McGrath, a Protestant himself, nevertheless, states, "Protestant justification involves the alien righteousness of Christ imputed to the believer, *external to him, not* located *in him*, or in any way *belonging* to him" (*Justitia Dei*). Verification of this can be noted in a quote from D. Martyn Lloyd-Jones, the popular Welsh preacher, "Justification makes *no actual change* in us; it is a declaration. ... The Christian is not a good man; he is a vile wretch saved by the grace of God." (*Romans: Atonement and Justification*, Pg. 55). More recently, we have the comment of John Macarthur, "Justification effects *no actual change* whatsoever in the sinner's nature or character. Justification is a divine judicial edict. It changes our status only..." (*www.newtestament-christian.com*). This kind of thinking is what caused the post-reformation Catholic theologians to chide the Protestants by indicating that "if a Protestant were ever to act righteously, he would have to attribute such to human 'works,'" for Protestant theology makes no provision for the subjective resource of the divine dynamic of the righteousness of the indwelling Christ. Such a charge galled the Protestants whose whole objective was to avoid "works righteousness." But these foregoing quotations reveal the foundation of the problem we confront today in articulating the subjective-particulars of the gospel and the indwelling presence of Christ and His righteousness.

Though my personal ministry has emphasized the subjective-particular of the human response of faith, initially and continuously, as well as the indwelling presence of the living Lord Jesus that facilitates a spiritual union with Christ whereby He is our life, let us never forget that the subjective-particular must be founded on the bedrock of what God has done objectively in the Person of Jesus, historically documentable and theologically explained. Otherwise the entire gospel message loses its moorings, is tossed to and from like the waves of the sea creating emotional froth. We become myopic and anthropocentric, man-centered instead of Christ-centered, and less concerned about others than ourselves.

The balanced tension of this dialectic must be maintained!

A Comprehensive Dialectic

It will now be instructive to return to an overview of the dialectic between the objective-universal and the subjective-particular wherein we see that the "extent and efficacy of the life and work of Jesus Christ" applies to ALL and yet NOT ALL. This is a very complex and comprehensive dialect that is inclusive of many distinctions, so we will add other words and phrases to the diagram in order to better see and understand the contrasts. (*cf. Addendum I*)

Before we do so, let me remind you that this kind of both/and dialectic that we are considering is difficult for our minds to accommodate. It is difficult to see both sides of a coin simultaneously without focusing on one side and causing the other side to be out of sight. But we do not want to look at one side of a coin and deny that the other side exists. This kind of dialectic demands that we keep the truth-tenets side-by-side without attempting to logically force one *into* or *apart from* of the other. They are both in a necessary relation to the other, requiring a balanced-tension between them. This is not an Hegelian dialectic between thesis and antithesis with an objective to create a synthesis that fuses the two. This is a tensioned dialectic that requires each side to balance the other and provide interactive explanation for the other.

In the diagram we are considering here (*cf. Addenum I*) we are just attempting to gain some perspective of the comprehensiveness of our dialectic, and to see some of the contrasts that are included within these two categories.

• The objective-universal ALL and the subjective-particular NOT ALL is a recognition of the tension that Christians from the earliest days of the Christian faith have weighed and pondered between *God's sovereign activity* and *man's response-ability*. (Note that we hyphenated the word as response-ability, rather than referring to "responsibility" which has developed the connotation of duty and obligation performed by self-effort.)

• The objective explains the "*indicative*" of God's action – He has done what He has done, because He IS who He is! Whereas the subjective includes the *imperative* of human response, wherein God always provides the dynamic of His own demands.

• In the objective-universal column we have placed the word "Grace" – God's action consistent with His character, while in the subjective-particular column we have the word "faith" – our receptivity of His activity – the freely-chosen consent of human individuals.

• Objectively, God has done what He has done in His Son Jesus Christ **for** us, on our behalf. He didn't even consult us, nor was it contingent on our consent. But subjectively, God continues to work **in** us, indicating that His GRACE is operative in both columns.

• The objective involves what God has effected and enacted outside of us, whereas subjectively we allow what God has effected to be personally experienced within us.

• From the cross Jesus declared triumphantly, *tetelesai*, "It is finished!" The objective of God is hereby accomplished, set in motion, sufficient to redeem and restore humanity. Yet, subjectively, we participate in the process of salvation and sanctification, whereby the "saving life" of the once-and-for-all Savior is worked out with our consent of faith.

• Objectively, the extent and efficacy of the life and work of Jesus Christ is effected historically and explained theologically, but subjectively we experience the personal and relational life and work of Jesus Christ wherein we know that we are loved, and we feel the embrace of His grace.

• Objectively, the Last Adam, Jesus Christ represented ALL men. We were "in Him" as He took our place in death. Everyone of us was included. It was not contingent on our consent. It was sort of like an arranged marriage, an arranged union. But thank God we have the opportunity of an intimate and personal relationship and union with the living Christ, subjectively – a participatory experience with the Triune God, Father, Son and Holy Spirit.

• The objective side involved the whole of collective humanity, the entire human race. But as individual human beings we are joined to the living Jesus and become "one spirit" (I Cor. 6:17) with Him. Jesus did what He did for ALL men, but He did what He did for "you" and for "me," and provides everything necessary for us to be the person God intends us to be!

This more comprehensive listing of the dialectic is an attempt to provide a perspective of the broad spectrum of contrasting concepts involved in what we are discussing.

There are those who have and will decry or object to the categories of "objective" and "subjective" being used in this dialectic explanation to explain what transpires *external* to us and what takes place *internally* within the Christian. Their complaint often is, "These words are not in Bible, and we find them confusing." One's response might be, "Well, the words "Trinity" and "rapture" are not in the Bible either, but Christians through the centuries have deemed them to be helpful for biblical interpretation and understanding. The failure to differentiate what occurs *outside* of us and what happens *inside* of us has led to a mess of muddled ambiguity within Christian discussion over the centuries, and has often led to divisive misunderstandings. It is important to make these kinds of distinctions.

This terminology of "objective" (external) and "subjective" (internal) is nothing new. It has been used in educated discussion for millennia. (*cf. Addendum J*) The Greek philosophers Plato and Aristotle used these concepts, as have subsequent philosophers and theologians and common Christians through the ages who have sought to clarify what they want to say. Major philosophical and theological thinkers can be contrasted by whether they tended to emphasize the objective or the subjective, often differentiated philosophically between "realism" and "personalism." Early theologians, Augustine and Thomas Aquinas, sided with Plato and Aristotle, respectively. Rene Descartes (1596-1650) and Immanuel Kant (1724-1804) emphasized the subject-personalist perspective, whereas G.W.F. Hegel (1770-1831) emphasized the objective-realist perspective. Aligned with Augustinian thought, the reformers, Martin Luther and John Calvin, focused on the objective-universal, but the Christian philosophers, Georg Hamann (18th century), Soren Kierkegaard (19th century), and John MacMurray (20th century), countered the reformers (theologically) and Hegel (philosophically) by emphasizing the subjective-personal. Twentieth century theology was dominated by Karl Barth, and subsequently by Scottish theologian, T.F. Torrance, both writing from an objective-realist starting point. On the subjective-personalist side we have the Protestant thought and writings of W. Ian Thomas and Norman P. Grubb, as well as the Roman Catholic thought of Pope John Paul II and Pope Benedict XVI. Human thinkers have found it very difficult to maintain a tensioned balance.

Differing Christian communities and traditions have over the centuries tended to emphasize either the objective or subjective facets of Christ's life and work. Some Lutherans, for example, have tended to emphasize the objective-universal, as did the Swiss theologian, Karl Barth, and the broad theological wake influenced by his teaching. The numerous varieties of Wesleyans and Baptists have tended to emphasize the subjective-particular, as have the "evangelicals" of the twentieth and twenty-first centuries. Both perspectives must be maintained in order to retain a biblical balance.

To this point we have been constructing the framework or infrastructure for what I set out to address when I began this study. We have laid the foundational biblical and theological framework of this dialectic of the ALL and the NOT ALL, attempting to provide adequate biblical documentation for both theses. Now, we must proceed to consider the aberrations that can occur (and have occurred) when a balanced tension is not maintained between the objective-universal and the subjective-particular. That is what prompted my engagement in this study in the first place.

Particularism

We will first consider what happens when the objective-universal tenets are diminished or denied, and the particularization of the NOT ALL is theoretically developed in a manner that fails to maintain the dialectic balance. The either-or particularization can become polarized in the aberration of "Particularism." We have divided the particularist ideas into two categories: Objective Particularism and Subjective Particularism. These can also be identified with the alternative designations of Calvinist Particularism and Humanist Particularism. (*cf. Addendum K*)

Objective Particularism

Objective Particularism doesn't really fit into this dialectic diagram. It is a denial of both the objective-universal and the subjective-particular elements of the dialectic we have considered, and is therefore outside of the parameters of a biblically balanced theology as we have attempted to diagram.

It is a form of particularism, in that this system of thought recognizes that there is an either-or particularization wherein NOT ALL are identified with Christ as Christians, but they do not believe that this is subjectively determined by an individual's choice of faith. In the other column of the dialectic, they deny the universal implications of Christ's life and work, but accept the fact that God does work objectively, outside of the human person. So, taking a portion of each category, they posit that God *objectively* determines the *particularity* of whether an individual person is a recipient of the life and work of Jesus Christ or not – "objective particularism." This strange and peculiar amalgam of thought is an anomaly to the dialectic that we have attempted to thoroughly document from the inspired scriptures.

This system of thought we are identifying as "objective particularism" was initially articulated in the 4th century with the thought and writings of Augustine of Hippo (A.D. 354-430). As a young adult Augustine espoused the religion of Manichaeism, a religion that began in Persia and incorporated ideas from Zoroastrianism, along with Greek Gnosticism, attempting to merge these with Christian thought. Manichaeism began in the 3rd century with a teacher named Mani, and central to his teaching was a dualist premise of good and evil. The human being, particularly the physical body and sexual function, was essentially evil, and the adherents of Manichaeism engaged in strict practices to identify with the good and achieve the level of being the "elect." After almost a decade in Manichaeism, Augustine decided that his own lascivious lifestyle and sinful proclivities (he had a mistress and they had a son) were not suited to the strict practices of this religion, and he moved to Italy where he could pursue a teaching career in rhetoric. In Milan he associated himself with Ambrose, a Christian bishop whose theology attempted to combine the Platonic dualism of the Greek philosopher, Plotinus, with Christian thought – an adaptation of Gnosticism – which conveniently coincided in large part with his previous Manichaean thinking.

From this background Augustine developed the anthropological thesis that when humanity fell into sin "in Adam," all human beings became, not only affected by, but guilty of, Adam's sin, and the very "being" of human being became defective, debased, degraded and deviant. The *essentia humanum*, the essential factors of humanness that we identified earlier: 1) spiritual, psychological, and physiological function, 2) humanity's derivation from a spiritual source, and 3) human self-determination via freedom of choice; these were all denied by Augustine. Instead of the tri-fold function of spirit, soul and body, the human person was viewed as a dualistic composition of a soul inside of a body seeking to escape into a heavenly existence. Instead of human beings functioning as spiritually derivative individuals, fallen human beings were regarded as having a spiritual vacuum necessitating psychological function as an autonomous "independent self" inflicted with an inherently depraved character of evil. Instead of self-determination via freedom of choice, human psychological faculties were deemed to be faulty and impaired, rendering every human person incapable of any response to God and His action in Jesus Christ by an intrinsic "bondage of the will." The fall of humanity into sinfulness by the sin of Adam rendered humans sub-human. According to Augustine there was an ontological reductionism whereby humanity was vitiated, reduced in value and function, without any capability of response to the actions that the Creator God might undertake on their behalf in His Son, Jesus Christ. Augustine's Manichaeistic understanding of fallen mankind being essentially evil was only slightly modified by attribution of an "original sin" corruption emanating from the original man, Adam.

Such an anthropological perspective of despoiled and incapacitated humanity provided the logical correlate to a theology of divine determinism whereby the Almighty God of the universe necessarily acts objectively to provide remediation to the dilemma of a defective, deficient and substandard humanity. In reaction to his Manichaeistic background, Augustine realized that God was not in a dualistic stalemate or stand-off with evil, but was the omnipotent God of the universe who determined in eternity-past to overcome evil. Augustine's perspective of God was primarily that of a power-based, deterministic deity whose Free Will to self-determine and self-implement could not be limited, even by Himself, and His divine actions could not be countered or stopped. All God determines God implements; All God purposes God accomplishes. The explanation of this absolute, unmitigated, and irresistible power of God was later encompassed in the non-biblical word "sovereignty" – applied to God and His actions.

As an aside, let it be noted that this theological concept of "sovereignty" became the pivot point for later Augustinian theological formulations. A. W. Pink, for example, states, "The doctrine of God's sovereignty lies at the foundation of Christian theology." J. M. Boice writes, "The doctrine of the sovereignty of God is the doctrine that gives means and substance to all other doctrines." Is it not interesting that the *King James Bible* never uses the words "sovereign" or "sovereignty?" But the twentieth century *New International Version* uses the words "sovereign" or "sovereignty" on 297 occasions, with most of those being references to God. I consider it abominable when people presume to interpolate their theology into the text of scripture!

Employing this idea of a supreme, ascendant, unlimited and indisputable God, Augustine applied this power-based perspective of God to his anthropological concept of an ontologically corrupt and functionally incapacitated fallen humanity. Recognizing that the scriptures indicated an either-or particularity among men, Augustine surmised that in the divine fore-counsels of eternity-past God objectively predetermined and predestined the particularity of those who would be His "elect" and those who would be "non-elect." NOT ALL human beings were intended by God to be redeemed or saved. "Some men...are predestined unto everlasting life, and others foreordained to everlasting death" (*Westminster Confession* – chpt. 3, art. 3-5; chpt. 10, art. 2). Predestination of any kind is always double-predestination! Those human beings predestined to be damned are said to suffer the just and deserved consequence of their guilt for Adam's sin, while the predestined "elect" are the recipients of God's "sovereign grace" for eternity. This is the "objective-particularism" to which we refer.

Fast-forward more than a millennium, some 1100 years to the 16th century, and we discover that the Christian faith that survived the Dark Ages is predominantly articulated in Augustinian terms, for Augustine was the most prolific writer of the early centuries of the church and his books were those studied by Christian theologians throughout the centuries. In Germany there arose a reformer, Martin Luther, trained as an Augustinian monk, who reacted against the practices of the Roman Catholic Church and their works-oriented explanation of justification, but he retained, for the most part, the anthropological and theological presuppositions of his Augustinian training. From France came another reformer, John Calvin, another devotee of Augustinian thought (as almost all Roman Catholics of that day were), who fine-tuned Augustine's thought in his *Institutes of the Christian Religion* (1536), quoting Augustine over 400 times. Trained as a lawyer, John Calvin brought a carefully defined legal, juridical and forensic paradigm of thought to Augustine's divinely deterministic theology, particularly in the area of soteriology. He explained that the sins of the "elect" are imputed to Christ, and the divinely determined "elect" are imputed with the legal righteousness of Christ the Savior. God, the divine Judge, declares the "elect ones" to be righteous by the righteous work of Christ, and imputes the righteousness work of Christ to their account so that their status and standing before God is now reckoned to be righteous.

After John Calvin's death in 1564, much of the church in Western Europe adopted his adapted Augustinian theological thought. In the early 17th century, responding to the Dutch *Articles of Remonstrance* (1610), the Synod of Dort (1619) developed a summation of Calvinist thought that was later formed into the acrostic T.U.L.I.P., the basis of what is often called "five point Calvinism." The TULIP acrostic stands for: Total Depravity, Unconditional Election, Limited Atonement, Irresistible Grace, and Perseverance of the Saints. (*cf. Addendum L*)

It will be instructive to look at these letters of the TULIP in light of our previous explanation of Augustinian thought. (*cf. Addendum M*) What the TULIP signifies is the:

T otality of human faculties rendered corrupt, depraved, deficient, and defective.

Many have mistakenly thought that "total depravity" referred to the totality of the human race affected with a spiritual condition of spiritual depravity as a result of Adam's original sin, which would be a biblical premise. That is not what the "T" represents. In complete contrast to our prior explanation of human function, of the *essentia humanum* of tri-fold function, derivative function, and determinative function, wherein human beings are dependent, contingent, and receptive persons who derive character from a spiritual source, either God or Satan, and possess meaningful freedom of choice in their relation to God and to other human beings, Augustinian-Calvinism advocates an ontological deterioration, deformation, and degeneration of human nature, rendering humanity essentially evil and capable only of generating sinful character and behavior, while unable and incapable of any psychological or spiritual function whereby they might respond to God and His action in Jesus Christ. Such a thesis necessarily disallows the entire column of humanity's "subjective-particular" response-ability to God's action in Christ.

U ncontional selection of certain

individuals by a power-based deterministic deity.

Whereas the "T" premise explained the
Augustinian-Calvinist view of anthropology, the "U"
premise establishes their theology, their explanation of
a "power-based deterministic deity," a "sovereign God"
who makes the objective determination of particularity
between human individuals by selecting and
predestining some to be His "elect," destined to
everlasting life as Christians and an eternal heavenly
destiny, while others are predestined to be the "non-
elect," condemned to death for sharing the guilt of
Adam's sin and destined to the perdition of everlasting
damnation. Such divinely determined and implemented
objective particularization of the human race is a logical
extension of the "total depravity" that allegedly renders
man incapable of responding to God with "freedom of
choice," and obviously disallows for any condition of a
human response of faith to Christ's life and work,
instead attributing "faith" to be a "gift of God" given to
the "elect," but withheld from the non-elect.

L imited extent and efficacy of Jesus' work – only for the predetermined "elect."

Whereas the "T" and the "U" premises indicated the anthropological and theological stances of this "objective particularism" of Augustinian-Calvinism, the "L" premise explains their soteriological position. The limitation of the extent and efficacy of Jesus' life and work of redemption and salvation as only effectual for the predetermined "elect" of God is obviously a denial and rejection of the "objective-universal" thesis of the dialectic we have explicated. In this system of thought Jesus did not die for ALL human beings, but only for ALL of the elect – a qualified limitation of the ALL in this closed-system of "objective particularism." The atoning work of Christ that effects the at-one-ment of objective reconciliation between God and humanity is not available to ALL human beings, but is only available to those particular individuals preselected and "elected" by God's eternal and sovereign will.

I rresistible action of God's grace to compel the "elect" to faith and impute/ impose the benefits of Jesus Christ.

As a consistent logical consequence of the foregoing anthropological ("T"), theological ("U"), and soteriological ("L") premises, it follows that the sovereign irresistible grace-action of God would necessarily be activated to implement His predetermined selection of the "elect" to be the beneficiaries of the redemptive and atoning work of Jesus Christ. Being incapable of a self-determined faith-choice response, and unable to resist or reject God's choice of them, the preselected "elect" human individuals are of necessity irresistibly drawn by the all-powerful, sovereign grace-action of God into an objective reconciliation with God. This inevitable imposition or coercive compulsion of the "elect" is allegedly accomplished by a God-given faith within the human will that links with the irresistible God-enacted grace operative in Jesus Christ, whereby God legally imputes or coercively imposes the benefits of Jesus Christ on the "elect." Without human response-ability, and whether or not they desire or choose to do so, the prior elected and predestined individuals will be made to become Christians.

P erseverance of the compelled "elect," disallowing permanent relapse and ensuring heavenly destiny.

When the divinely elected individuals have been compelled to become Christians by the sovereign, all-powerful "irresistible grace" of God, they remain in a condition of "total depravity," incapable of response-ability towards God and His continuing activity – they are just "sinners saved by grace." God's all-powerful sovereign-grace action is therefore employed to cause His divinely selected and faith-imbued Christians to endure and persevere in their fidelity as God preserves them in their saved condition until death, disallowing any relapse and ensuring their divinely-determined eternal destiny in heaven – "once saved, always saved!"

This explanation of TULIP theology sufficiently summarizes the anomaly of "objective particularism," or the teaching that can also be termed "Augustinian-Calvinist particularism." Let it be noted that such Augustinian-Calvinist theology has had a prominent and significant impact on both Roman Catholic and Protestant Christian thought through the centuries and survives to this very day, but less of an influence on Eastern Orthodox doctrine.

Subjective Particularism

We must move on to consider the "subjective particularism" that often results from a neglect or failure to give adequate import to the "objective-universal" realities of the extent and efficacy of the life and work of Jesus Christ, while simultaneously over-emphasizing the human response-ability to subjectively particularize oneself in identification with Jesus Christ. This emphasis on the action of the human individual is the reason why "subjective particularism" can also be termed "humanist particularism," for the emphasis is put on what a *human being* does rather than on what

God has done and continues to do via the Son, Jesus Christ, and by the power of the Holy Spirit.

Whereas the "objective particularism" identified above modified the "objective universal" of the dialectic by diminishing the ALL and qualifying the ALL to mean "ALL those deterministically elected," this category of "subjective particularism" similarly diminishes and qualifies the ALL of the "objective particular" by constricting the ALL to refer to "ALL who respond to the gospel in accord with acceptable prescribed human actions," whether initially or throughout the Christian life.

In the 5th century in North Africa a polemic of theological ideology arose between Augustine (A.D. 354-430) and Pelagius (A.D. 354-440). The dispute centered on the "particularism" of the involvement of human individuals in the extent and efficacy of the life and work of Jesus Christ. Augustine subscribed to a divine determinism of "objective particularism" (as noted above), whereas Pelagius advocated a "subjective particularism" whereby each individual was regarded as an innocent, independent being with "free will," capable of self-determining and self-implementing either good or evil character, and able to choose the option of allowing Jesus to be one's Savior, with subsequent obedience to the gospel. Pelagianism is a radical example of subjective self-chosen human action that allegedly effects or causes the particularization by which an individual establishes his own personal salvation to become a Christian. Given the vehement polarization of Augustinianism and Pelagianism through the centuries of Christian thought, both extremes will be aghast to discover they are but variant forms of aberrant particularism.

Approximately 1200 years after the flap between Augustine and Pelagius, and about 70 years after John Calvin had soteriologically adapted Augustine's theology into a legal structure in his *Institutes of the Christian Religion* (1536), the followers of the Dutch Reformed theologian, Jacobus Arminius (A.D. 1560-1609) articulated their objection to Augustinian-Calvinist theology in the *Five Articles of Remonstrance* (1610), countering the five points that later became the Calvinist TULIP. Arminianism was not radically humanistic, as was Pelagianism, and often maintained the balance of the dialectic we have explicated, but variations of Arminianism tended to emphasize the necessity of human obedience and performance, lapsing into legalism and developing theological expressions that failed to adequately emphasize the grace of God in the Christian life.

In the past few centuries, beginning in the 17th century, a broad range of Christians has identified themselves as "evangelicals." The term is derived from the Greek word *euangellion*, meaning "good news" or "gospel." When used consistently with its linguistic meaning the term "evangelical" should indicate Christians who maintain a balanced perspective of the gospel, both of the "objective universal ALL" and the "subjective-particular NOT ALL" of the extent and efficacy of the life and work of Jesus Christ. But inevitably the meaning of terms naturally evolve as they interact with historical and cultural circumstances, and by the latter part of the 20th century the label "evangelical" had developed some general connotations. Distinctive features of "evangelicalism" included 1) the need for personal conversion or being 'born again," 2) a high regard for biblical authority, viewing the scriptures as the "word of God," 3) an emphasis on the atonement in the saving death and resurrection of Jesus Christ, and 4) active and concerted efforts of evangelism and social concern. David Bebbington referred to this "quadrilateral of priorities" of contemporary "evangelicalism" as "conversionism, Biblicism, crucicentrism, and activism" (*Evangelicalism in Modern Britain*. 1989. Pgs 2-17)

Evangelicalism is prominent in the present expression of American Christianity, but it has increasingly moved toward myriad forms of "subjective particularism" which emphasize human action referent to salvation and sanctification in both ecclesial and social contexts. Francis Schaeffer warned evangelicals about this in his 1984 book, *The Great Evangelical Disaster*. A decade later (1993) David Wells wrote *No Place for Truth: Whatever Happened to Evangelical Thought?* Mark Noll contributed to the discussion in a book entitled, *The Scandal of the Evangelical Mind* (1994).

The Philippians jailor frantically asked, "What must I do to be saved?" Paul and Silas responded, "Believe in the Lord Jesus Christ and you will be saved" (Acts 16:31). The question among evangelicals today is not whether they *believe* or not – the real question is what (or better Who) they believe in? Are they receptive to the living Lord Jesus and willing to be incorporated into His life to the extent that His life becomes the "saving life" of their life? Do evangelicals believe in the Triune God who revealed Himself in the Son, Jesus Christ, who by His objective-universal "finished work" has accomplished and continues to implement everything necessary for the restoration of humanity?

The aberration of evangelical*ism* has often tended to drift towards belief in experience, whether a conversion experience, a baptismal experience (water baptism or Spirit baptism), or an ecstatic or ecclesial experience that is often a demonstration of emotionalism. It is a distinctive of evangelicalism to emphasize belief in the Bible, elevating the book and its literalistic interpretation to a place of saving importance in a Biblicism that verges on Bibliolatry. With their intense emphasis on "faith" as the human response-action, evangelicals may tend toward "faith in faith," a fideism wherein individual faith is alleged to save a person. Faith in human belief-systems is another trap for evangelicals as they formulate their particular form of believe-right religion in the accuracy of apologetics and the correct doctrines of fundamentalism. At the core of evangelicalism has been the emphasis on conversionism, decisionism, and revivalism whereby individuals are encouraged to "get saved" in a punctiliar event of "instant salvation" by raising their hand, walking an aisle, coming to the altar, saying a "sinner's prayer," or exercising an ideological option to make a "decision for Christ" (ex. Billy Graham Evang. Assoc., *Decision* magazine). Evangelical faith is often cast in categories of morality and ethics that form a do-right religion closely monitored in legalism, with repetitive inculcations to human betterment via behavior modification. Belief in prophetic fulfillment has had a large place in evangelicalism, with speculative explanations of dispensationalism, millennialism, and eschatological futurism.

Evangelicals have often attempted to marry their religious faith to nationalism and patriotism, creating a civil religion of Americanism, preaching democratic freedom and liberty in a highly combative politicism. Many evangelicals have been caught up in the sectarianism of denominationalism, advocating the status-quo of traditionalism. Other evangelicals have focused their belief on supernaturalism, on signs and wonders and miracles of tongues and healings in Pentecostalism or charismaticism. Such an emphasis on ecstatic anti-intellectualism that eschews rationality is countered by those who would employ rationalist enlightenment thought in forms of Gnosticism and propositionalism – religious knowledge whores. The evangelical emphasis on human "belief" has led to constant arguments of theological correctness in Calvinism versus Arminianism. When evangelicals have integrated their belief with the church, they have emphasized the quantitative enlargement of statistical success in the "bigger is better" motif of the "church growth movement." Or, more lately, in the personalism and relationalism of the "emergent church movement."

When it comes to their interaction with the culture around them, evangelicals have often chosen extremes of social passivism or social activism, either advocating withdrawal from the world in a sacred-secular dichotomy tending to separatism or isolationism ("why polish brass on a sinking ship" –

141

J. Vernon McGee), or seeking to change the culture by social and political power plays on such social issues as abortion, euthanasia, pornography via the "religious right," "moral majority" or the "values clarification" movement. More often than not, though, evangelicalism has tended to adapt to the culture around them in the pragmatism of accomodationism, seeking to be relevant in a cultural relativism.

One segment of evangelicalism has focused their belief on the interiority of immanentism or private pietism, referring to a "higher life" or a "deeper life" or an "exchanged life" wherein an individual's faith should just "let go, and let God" do as He will in an experiential free-fall. Integrating psychological thought with their faith, some evangelicals have focused their belief in "knowing who they are" by asserting their perceived new identity *in* Christ or *as* Christ, which can result in an idolatrous self-deification. If caution is not exercised, evangelicals can end up believing in themselves more than they believe in Jesus, in a form of narcissistic individualism and "me-ism," wherein "it's all about me" – *my* spirituality, *my* holiness, *my* growth and *my* discipleship.

Evangelical emphasis on human action so easily deteriorates into the religionism of self-justification by means of the religious performance of self-effort, falling into the "works" mentality that Protestantism originally reacted to. Performance-oriented religion with its calls for "you oughta, you gotta" do this or that, and with its "how-to" admonitions for commitment, dedication and increased consecration has created an "evangelical humanism" among American Christians. Even to the extent that they regard their humanly enacted religious efforts with a sense of achievement, and often with a sense of entitlement to God's "benefits" of salvation, well-being, and heavenly destiny.

This is a dangerous place to be – to insist that human actions have a meritorious effect towards our own salvation – to think that we can command or demand God to act on our behalf. Evangelicalism has certainly tilted into the aberration of "subjective particularism" when we regard our human actions as placing any kind of contingency on God's actions – when we fail to affirm that the "objective-universal" acts of God in the "finished work" of Jesus Christ have effected everything necessary for the salvation of mankind. Our "faith" does not save us – Jesus Christ saves us by His historic redemptive life and work and His continued restorative life and work – and the human response of "faith" simply receives the Savior.

Many evangelicals have been camped-out in the category of the "subjective-particular" for so long, emphasizing what human beings are responsible for before God, that when they hear the declarations of the "objective-universal" realities of Christ's life and work completely accomplished on their behalf, and requiring no effort or co-operation on their part, these statements sound strange and foreign to their ears. In fact, they may adjudge them to be heretical false teaching. Those who neglect or deny the "objective-universal" foundation of what God has done in Christ for ALL men are in grave danger of building their thought-edifice on the shifting sands of subjectivity, with an undue emphasis on human action rather than God's actions.

Those of us who have identified ourselves as "evangelicals" may need to be self-evaluative, or even self-critical, at this point, considering whether our focus has truly been on the Evangel, on the One who is in Himself the "good news" of the gospel, and has given

Himself entirely "once and for all" to take the death consequences of our sin and to provide His divine Life to ALL mankind. The need of evangelicalism today is not a new revival – not a new reformation – not better methods for "doing church" – the need is for a balanced perspective of the "objective-universal" alongside of the "subjective-particular" of the extent and efficacy of the life and work of Jesus Christ.

Universalism

Having now considered the aberrant extreme of "Particularism" in the forms of both "objective particularism" and "subjective particularism," we now proceed to consider the aberrant extreme of "universalism" on the other side of the dialectic diagram. (*cf. Addendum N*) When the "objective-universal" realities of the comprehensive Person and work of Jesus Christ are emphasized without an adequate counter-emphasis on the "subjective-particular" means of human response and experience, then an inevitable slide toward universalism is the result. A generic form of determined universalism is operative whenever all the objects of a defined group are categorically included in an action or grouping, without any option for individuated inclusion or exclusion. So, when the human response-ability of choice is diminished or denied, some form of deterministic universalism is necessarily imposed on the whole of humanity.

Universalism, in general, appears to many to be such a natural, inclusive, non-judgmental, loving concept. I can recall when I was in the 2nd or 3rd grade of elementary school, and everyone in the class was required to memorize and recite a poem. I found a short poem in one of my mother's books, and I can still quote that poem to this day:

> "He drew a circle that shut me out.
> Heretic, rebel, a thing to flout.
> But love and I had the wit to win.
> We drew a circle that took him in."

The words of this poem entitled "Outwitted" by Edwin Markham seem so inclusive and the naturally right thing to do, and it was only later in life that I realized that the poem can be understood to advocate a form of relativistic "universalism" that discourages the drawing of lines that distinguish one thing from another. Are there not ideas in life where we are obliged to "draw a line in the sand" to delineate what we might regard as non-negotiable issues? Do we want to come to the point where we are "beyond heresy," and can no longer draw a line between orthodoxy and heresy? Do "love and I" (is the poem talking about God?) always have the "wit to

win, by drawing a circle that takes the other in,"
regardless of their positions or behavior? Rhetorical
questions to ponder, but we must move on, beyond the
poetic fancies.

Prior to considering the historical background of
general universalist thought, let us note that there is an
anomaly on the side of universalism, just as there was in
the consideration of particularism. Augustinian-
Calvinist thought proposed an *"objective particularism"*
that was outside of the parameters of the dialectic being
studied. There is also a form of *"subjective universalism"*
that similarly does not fit into the dialectic between the
"objective-universal" and the "subjective-particular."
This category of thought asserts that all human beings
will sooner or later come to the subjective realization
that we are all worshipping the same god, whatever
name we might call it. This god, whoever she might be,
must be a gracious, loving god who could not/would not
consign any creatures to misery or discomfort, must
less to perdition or hell. In the end ALL human beings
will be included in the presence of God whatever that
might entail. We are all in the same boat that is going to
the same place, so all human particularizations of

thought or religion, etc. are irrelevant, and we all just need to learn how to meld and to merge, to integrate and assimilate, and to all "get along" in world peace. This kind of inclusivist and universalistic monism is apparent in many Eastern religions.

In a more Christian context this "subjective universalism" may take the form of emphasizing that Jesus is "the true light that lighteth every man" (Jn. 1:9-KJV) from within, inherently and intrinsically. Since all human persons are "spirit-beings" with the "inner light" deep inside, the need amongst men is simply to become aware of their common enlightenment. Admittedly, some individuals just seem to be more tuned-in to their inner spiritual reality than others, and they have become "spiritual knowers" by the light of "inner revelation," aware of who they really are in Christ, and to help others "see the light." Some branches of "Union Life" teaching have advocated such "subjective universalism."

Needless to say, such "subjective universalism" sounds rather like pie-in-the-sky gibberish about utopian pipe-dreams to most thinking people. Perhaps equally as foreign to logical and biblical reasoning as the "objective particularism" advocated by Augustinian-Calvinism. They are both outside of the parameters of the dialectic we are considering.

Another almost oxymoronic variety of thought should be interjected at this point. There are some who have attempted to subsume the entire category of human subjective response within the objective universal actions of God in Jesus Christ. In this form of universal objective-subjective all of the subjective actions of the Person of Jesus Christ are regarded as having been made vicariously "in the place of" the subjective responses of all human persons. They identify this as the "vicarious humanity" of Jesus Christ.

Under the general heading of "universalism," we will be considering the two categories – "general universalism" and "deterministic universalism." Under "general universalism" we will consider a brief historical review of how the universalistic thesis of the ultimate and eventual reconciliation and restoration of all mankind, universally, in a right relationship with God has arisen in association with Christian thought throughout the centuries. Our primary focus, though, will be on the particular form of "deterministic universalism" that has become prominent in recent years. I mentioned this almost a decade ago in an article, "Universalism: It's Forms and Fallacies."

It is important to realize that any form of universalism necessarily fails to account for the human individual as a self-determinative being with free-choices that have real consequences. Universalism denies or refuses to consider the "subjective-particular."

General Universalism

There has been a long history of universalist thought throughout the history of the Christian faith. It has not always been explicit, but leanings toward some form of universalism can be detected in the writings of numerous individuals in church history. As early as the Alexandrian school in Egypt in the 2nd century, there are intimations of inclusiveness wherein all human persons will eventually be perfected in the eternal presence of God. Clement of Alexandria (150-220) may have espoused such, as well as his student and successor, Origen Adamantius (185-254), for both have been cited with comments that might be considered universalistic.

Influenced by Origen's theological perspective, Gregory of Nyssa (335-394) wrote of "the annihilation of evil, the restitution of all things, and the final restoration of evil men and evil spirits to the blessedness of union with God, so that He may be 'all in all,' embracing all things endowed with sense and reason" (*Sermo Catecheticus Magnus*). Nestorius (386-451) and his followers, known as the Nestorians, who were instrumental in the development of the Assyrian Church of the East, seem to have had universalist leanings. As a result of the increasing popularity of Nestorian teaching, the concept of "universalism" was condemned as heretical in the Fifth General Council of the Church, convened at Constantinople, in A.D. 553.

Universalistic thought continued to crop up, however, in the thought and writing of the Scotch-Irish theologian, Johannes Scotus Erigena (815-877), as well as in the writings of Meister Eckhart (1260-1328) and Blessed John of Ruysbroek (1293-1381), who were both influential in the thinking of German Dominican preacher, Johannes Tauler (1300-1361). During the Reformation of the 16th century, a large and diverse group known as Anabaptists arose in Switzerland and

Germany, and some of them seemed to be inclined toward universalist thought. German missionary Peter Boehler (1712-1775) spread the Moravian faith to England and the American colonies, and his universalistic thought can be detected in his words, "all the damned souls shall yet be brought out of hell." The Quakers (aka the Society of Friends), began in England in the 17th century with George Fox as founder. They emphasized direct religious experience rather than sacraments or scriptural dogmatism, and taught that the "Inner Light," the Spirit of God, is within every person.

The German cobbler mystic, Jacob Boehme (1575-1624), had a universalist influence on the Anglican writer William Law (1686-1761). James Relly (1722-1778) was a Methodist minister from Wales who embraced the teaching of universal salvation, and served as a mentor to John Murray, the father of the Universalist Church of America.

In terms of the modern theology of the last couple of centuries, German theologian, Friedrich D. E. Schleiermacher (1768-1834) taught an explicit form of universalism. Countering the "limited atonement" of

Calvinism, he taught that all men are elected to salvation in Christ, and this divine purpose implemented by divine omnipotence cannot fail. Schleiermacher represents a form of Reformed or Calvinistic universalism, grounded in a power-based deterministic God.

In nineteenth-century England the problem of hell and universal salvation became a matter of widespread discussion. In 1853 F. D. Maurice was dismissed from his professional chair at King's College, London, for a cautious challenge of the traditional doctrine of hell. F. W. Farrar denied eternal punishment in a famous series of sermons in Westminster Abbey in 1877 (published as *Eternal Hope*, 1878). Scottish preacher and novelist, George MacDonald (1824-1905), reacted against the Calvinist concept of "limited atonement" in many of his writings, and thought it likely that all human beings would be transfigured by God's love.

Twentieth century theological thought was eclipsed by the massive contribution of Swiss Reformed theologian, Karl Barth (1886-1968), particularly in his thirteen-volume *magnum opus*, entitled *Church*

Dogmatics. Barth's unique perspective of Christology, wherein he seemed to indicate that all humanity is subsumed into the incarnational expression of the God-man, Jesus, became the basis for his soteriological thesis that Jesus was "the only reprobate man," as well as "the singular Elect Man" for all humanity, thus allowing for the life and work of Jesus Christ to serve as the reconciliation and restoration of all men to right relationship with God. This rejection of the Augustinian-Calvinist premise of "limited atonement" while retaining the presuppositional premises of a deterministic deity and deficient humanity, allows or compels the pendulum of Calvinist thought to swing to the opposite extreme of universalism, though Barth always denied being a "universalist."

Hans Urs Von Balthasar (1905-1988), a contemporary and friend of Karl Barth in Basel, was also a Swiss theologian, though within the Roman Catholic Church. He was not an explicit advocate of universalism, yet culminated his voluminous writing career by entertaining the question, *Dare We Hope "That All Men Be Saved"?* (1989), reserving the answer to God's mercy and mysteries.

A contemporary instance of explicit universalist thought can be found in the writings of Gary Amirault on his website: www.tentmaker.org.

We sum up this survey of the history of universalistic thought by returning to the previous mention of John Murray who first organized the Universalist Church in America. Born in England in a strict Calvinistic home, Murray was befriended as a teenager by John Wesley and became a Methodist preacher. Later he joined George Whitefield's evangelistic endeavors and in that context he met and joined in ministry with Welshman, James Relly, who had broken with Wesley and Whitefield over the teaching of universalism – denying the doctrine of eternal damnation, and advocating the ultimate restoration of all human souls in the eternal presence of God. After the death of his young wife, John Murray set sail to America and became a popular preacher of universalism. In 1793 the teaching of universalism emerged as an organized denomination in the United States, called the Universalist Church in America. Later, in 1961 the Universalist Church in America (UCA) united with the American Unitarian Association (AUA) to form the

Unitarian Universalist Association (UUA), which survives to this day, generally regarded as a hodge-podge association of liberal go-gooders without much substance.

Determinist Universalism

This historical review of general universalism as it has hovered around Christian thought through the centuries will now serve as a stepping stone for us to move on to the other category of universalism that we have identified – "Deterministic Universalism." You may have noticed that several Christian thinkers mentioned in the historical review of "general universalism" had reacted against the "determinist particularism" of the Calvinist-Reformed doctrine of "limited atonement" – Schleiermacher, George MacDonald, Karl Barth, John Murray, for example – and by various means of consideration their conclusions slid into the category that we are viewing – "determinist universalism."

To see how this can happen, let us wander back into the theological garden, and look again at the T.U.L.I.P. theology that summarizes the "objective particularism" of Augustinian-Calvinist determinism. What would happen if the "L" petal of the TULIP acrostic was plucked off? … and if we were to indicate that the "certain individuals" in the "U" petal was ALL individuals? Would this allow the TULIP theology to move into the categories of the dialectic we are considering of "the extent and efficacy of the life and work of Jesus Christ"? By dispensing with the "L" petal, and intimating that Jesus Christ lived and died for ALL men, these theological TULIP growers would move into alignment with the "objective universal" category of the dialectic, recognizing that the "extent and efficacy" of God's work in Jesus Christ was for ALL mankind. But when the "T," "U," "I," and "P" petals still deny and disallow human beings the opportunity of choosing to avail themselves of Christ's life and work in the "subjective particular" factor of the dialectic, the alleged defective human beings would remain incapable of responding to God's action.

With a slight mutation of the "L" (and maybe the "U") petal, they could make a genetically altered, modified variety of the TULIP flower – the "Evangelical-Calvinist TULIP." (*cf. Addendum O*)

T otality of human faculties rendered corrupt, depraved, deficient, and defective.

U nconditional election of humanity in the "Elect One," Jesus, by the power-based deterministic deity

L imitless extent and efficacy of Jesus' work – ALL humanity were substituted for in the "vicarious humanity" of Jesus

I rresistible action of God's grace to compel the "elect" to faith and impute/impose the benefits of Jesus Christ

P erseverance of the compelled "elect," disallowing permanent relapse and ensuring heavenly destiny.

Regrettably, this modified and mutated TULIP still does not conform completely to the parameters of a biblical understanding of the "extent and efficacy of the life and work of Jesus Christ." It still denies the human being the choice of receiving by faith what Christ has accomplished. And what happens when one side of the dialectic is emphasized to the denial of the other? It tilts into the aberration of over-emphasis, which in this case is "deterministic universalism." The Calvinist TULIP can be uprooted from just outside of the fence of the "good news" garden, in "objective-deterministic particularism," and replanted just outside of the fence on the other side of the garden, in "objective-deterministic universalism," but it still fails to qualify as a balanced expression of the gospel.

It was noted previously that the vast majority of the persons promulgating this theological paradigm had previously subscribed to the classic Calvinism of the 5-point TULIP. They made a big leap to jettison the idea of "limited atonement," the idea that the "extent and efficacy" of Jesus' death was only for selected "elect" individuals, and Jesus didn't die for the rest of humankind. It was a great shift of theological perspective to now advocate the statements of the "objective universal" of Christ's life and work for ALL humanity.

I determined that it was only fair to begin this study by noting some of the "objective universal" statements being espoused by these self-named "Evangelical Calvinists," – to at least list those that could be deemed to have some legitimate documentation in scripture, provided we accept the objective interpretation with which they view them. That is what I did!

Why, then, is it the evangelicals who get so riled up about the affirmation of "objective-universal" statements concerning the "extent and efficacy of the life and work of Jesus Christ"? Because they are, in large part, viewing the situation from the extremist perspective of "subjective particularism." When evangelicals allow themselves to slide into "Evangelical*ism*," they too have failed to stand in the biblical balance of the "objective-universal" and the "subjective-particular." So, from the precipice of their own aberration in "subjective particularism," they hurl charges and invectives across the chasm at those they have determined to be "heretical" over there in the aberration of "deterministic universalism." From ditch to ditch they fire their rocket salvos at one another, indicative of the religious wars that have raged throughout the centuries.

Whenever I attempt to be fair in presenting the listing of "objective-universal" affirmations, as I did earlier, it is the Evangelicals who often start to choke and cough and sputter and gag. And I have to admit that

I have not always interpreted the scriptures previously cited in an objective-universal sense either. I had to swallow hard a few times as I compiled the list. But I utilized the statements that seemed to me to have some basis of biblical justification and documentation when interpreted from an objective perspective.

But I must go on to explain that some of the more radical Deterministic Universalists don't stop there. They go beyond the list considered earlier (*cf. Addendum F*), and they include additional affirmations of the "objective-universal" implications of the life and work of Jesus Christ that seem to be far-reaching overstatements that go beyond the bounds of scriptural teaching.

For example, they might state (and have stated) the following premises: (*cf. Addenda P and Q*)

ALL HUMANITY ...

... is integrally united with God – the separation of sin is but an illusion of a depraved mind.

... is subsumed into God's being in the union of deity and humanity in the God-man, Jesus.

... is drawn into fellowship and participation with the Triune God via the humanity of Jesus.

... is granted access into the Holy of Holies of God's presence via Jesus.

... is replaced with the humanity of Christ before God. Jesus was the "Man for all man>"

... has been vicariously substituted for as Jesus was born, lived, and died "in our stead."

... is baptized into Christ – overwhelmed into Him by His assumption of our humanity.

... is "born again" by the incarnational birth of Jesus in the womb of Mary.

... is relationally "in Christ," i.e. has a relation with God by the life and work of Jesus.

... is a "new creature in Christ," for Jesus Christ has recreated humanity in Himself.

... has been transformed from being sub-human to being Christ-humans – a Christ-replaced humanity.

... has undergone an ontological exchange of being, nature, identity & character in union with Christ.

... is imputed with the entire character and being of Christ – human being has become Christ-being.

... is a Christ-instilled race – an ontologically altered race of human creatures.

... became "partakers of the divine nature" when the divine-human Jesus became the redemptive integrator of God and man.

... had the choice made for them, when Christ chose to become Man and live "as us."

... has exercised faith in God by the "faith of Christ" – Christ is the faith-er for all mankind.

... is considered obedient by God, by the obedience of Jesus Christ in our place. Jesus is the "Obedient One."

... prayerfully communes with God through the prayers of Jesus – Jesus is the pray-er for us.

... worships God the Father via the worship of Jesus Christ – Jesus is the worshipper as us.

... functions by the enlivening of Christ, for "in Him we live and move and have our being."

... functions by the provision of Christ, for "apart from Him, we can do nothing."

... has entered "eternal life" in Christ, and "are seated with Christ in the heavenlies."

... participates in the eternal heavenly destiny in Christ

... can disregard all the religious threats of hell – ain't no such place, and nobody's going there.

How many of these are you be willing to add to the list of objective-universals of the "extent and efficacy" of the life and work of Christ? I decided that there was insufficient biblical support to include these kinds of statements in the list of objective-universals.

When the aforementioned types of statements become part of one's theological platform, and when they explicitly deny the "subjective-particular" of human response-ability to respond to God's action in Jesus Christ by human faith, then the danger of sliding into "deterministic universalism" will necessarily present itself. Whenever Christian thinkers go beyond biblically defensible statements, and begin to employ philosophical theological presuppositions to interpret the scriptures in a different manner, they tilt away from the biblical balance of the dialectic we have considered. Whenever Christian thought fails to account for the balance between the "objective-universal" and the "subjective-particular," it will inevitably veer off into extremist aberration.

Conclusion

My purpose in this study has been to provide
some perspective on how differing theological systems
relate to the biblical tension of the dialectic between the
"objective-universals" of the ALL, and the "subjective-
particulars" of the NOT ALL concerning the "extent and
efficacy of the life and work of Jesus Christ."

The tensioned balance is difficult to maintain.
The tendency of all human thinkers, particularly those
of the Western world, is to find a "comfort zone" on one
side or the other of the dialectic, because we think in
terms of an *either-or* dichotomy rather than in the terms
of a *both-and* balance.

Given the difficulty of maintaining a biblical
balance, and recognizing that we are all just finite
creatures attempting to understand infinite realities, let
us be very cautious about hurling charges or invectives
against those who have a different emphasis that our
own. Regardless of where our brothers or sisters in
Christ have pitched their tent on this theological
landscape, we must seek to maintain the fellowship of

unity in the bond of love. Christians must always be willing to agree to disagree!

Bibliography of Cited Sources

Augustine, Aurelius, *On the Predestination of the Saints.*

Barclay, William, *The Mind of Saint Paul.*

Barth, Karl, *Church Dogmatics.*

Bebbington, David, *Evangelicalism in Modern Britain*

Berkouwer, G.C., Faith and Justification

Brunner, Emil, *Dogmatics Vol. III*

Bultman, Rudolph, *The Dictionary of New Testament Theology*, Article on "Faith"

Calvin, John, *Institutes of the Christian Religion.*

Capon, Robert. *Kingdom, Grace, Judgment: Paradox, Outrage, and Vindication in the Parables of Jesus.*

Farrar, F.W., *Eternal Hope.*

Five Articles of Remonstrance.

Graham, Billy, *Decision* magazine.

Gregory of Nazianzus, *Epistle 51 to Cledonius.*

Gregory of Nyssa, *Sermo Catecheticus Magnus.*

Hegel, Georg Wilhelm Friedrich, *Philosophy of Right*, "Theory of Marriage."

Kierkegaard, Soren, *Either/Or.*

Lewis, C.S., *Mere Christianity.*

Lewis, C.S., *The Great Divorce.*

Lloyd-Jones, D. Martyn, *Romans: Atonement and Justification.*

MacArthur, John, www.newtestament-christian.com

Machen, J. Gresham, *What is Faith?*

Markham, Edwin, "Outwitted"

Mascall, E.L., *Christ, the Christian, and the Church*

McGrath, Alister, *Justitia Dei.*

Merton, Thomas, *The New Man.*

Moffatt, James, *Grace in the New Testament.*

Murray, John, *Redemption – Accomplished and Applied*

Noll, Mark, *The Scandal of the Evangelical Mind.*

Pink, A.W., *The Sovereignty of God*

Schaeffer, Francis, *The Great Evangelical Disaster*

Thomas, W. Ian, taped message.

Thomas, W. Ian, *The Mystery of Godliness*

Von Balthasar, Hans Urs, *Dare We Hope "That All Men Be Saved?"*

Wells, David, *No Place for Truth: Whatever Happened to Evangelical Thought?*

Westminster Confession.

ADDENDA

The Extent
of the Life and

Universalism

Objective Universal
ALL

General Universalism

ALL of humanity is designed and destined to spend eternity in heaven

- This universal destiny has been pre-determined and is not predicated on any human response.

Determinist Universalism

ALL of humanity is deterministically sub-sumed into the incarna-tional life and ministry of Jesus Christ, and His "vicarious humanity" incorporates all human beings into His Being and action for eternity.

God's historic **GRACE** action in the life and work of His Son Jesus Christ is a "finished work" demonstrating:

ALL humanity loved by God

ALL humanity graced by God

ALL humanity elected in Christ

ALL humanity represented by Christ

ALL humanity died in Christ

ALL humanity redeemed in Christ

ALL humanity forgiven in Christ

ALL humanity reconciled in Christ

ALL humanity adopted in Christ

ALL humanity saved by Christ

ALL humanity given life in Christ

ALL humanity righteous in Christ

ALL humanity blessed in Christ

ALL humanity is "in Christ"

ALL humanity drawn to Christ

and Efficacy
Work of Jesus Christ

Subjective Particular
→ *NOT ALL*

The human individual's response-ability is to receive by **FAITH** what God has extended in His Son.

We learn to live loved.

We grow in the grace and knowledge

We are elect ones in the Elect One

We are united "one spirit" in Christ

We "reckon ourselves to be dead"

We live in the freedom of Christ

We accept God's forgiveness

We enjoy reconciled relationship

We cry "Abba Father! – adopted sons

We are being "saved by His life"

We affirm "Christ as our life"

We have become righteous in Christ

We have "every spiritual blessing"

We are "new creatures in Christ"

We draw near to the throne of grace

Particularism
→

Objective Particularism

ALL is qualified to mean "ALL of God's predetermined elect"

• God has determined some individuals to be His "elect"

• God has determined other individuals to be "non-elect"

Subjective Particularism

ALL is qualified to mean "ALL individuals who subjectively respond to the gospel of Jesus in faith and in accordance with the acceptable religious prescriptions."

173

The Extent
of the Life and

Universalism	Objective Universal *ALL* ←
General Universalism	ALL humanity loved by God
ALL of humanity is designed and destined to spend eternity in heaven	ALL humanity graced by God
	ALL humanity elected in Christ
• This universal destiny has been pre-determined and is not predicated on any human response.	ALL humanity represented by Christ
	ALL humanity died in Christ
	ALL humanity redeemed in Christ
	ALL humanity forgiven in Christ
	ALL humanity reconciled in Christ
Determinist Universalism	ALL humanity adopted in Christ
ALL of humanity is deterministically sub-sumed into the incarna-tional life and ministry of Jesus Christ, and His "vicarious humanity" incorporates all human beings into His Being and action for eternity.	ALL humanity saved by Christ
	ALL humanity given life in Christ
	ALL humanity righteous in Christ
	ALL humanity blessed in Christ
	ALL humanity is "in Christ"
	ALL humanity drawn to Christ

and Efficacy
Work of Jesus Christ

Subjective Particular
→ *NOT ALL*

Particularism

Biblical "theological anthropology."
- Tri-fold function
- Self-determinative function
  – "freedom of choice"
- Derivative function

Human response has NO merit.

Human response of FAITH.
- Faith is a human choice-action
- Faith is NOT a "work"
- Faith is NOT a "gift of God"
- "Our receptivity of His activity"

Either-or Particularization

Indwelling Divine Presence
- Christ in the Christian
- Divine Spirit working in Christian
- Ontological exchange
- Outworking of Christ's life

Objective Particularism

ALL is qualified to mean "ALL of God's predetermined elect"
- God has determined some individuals to be His "elect"
- God has determined other individuals to be "non-elect"

Subjective Particularism

ALL is qualified to mean "ALL individuals who subjectively respond to the gospel of Jesus in faith and in accordance with the acceptable religious prescriptions."

175

The Extent and Efficacy of the Life and Work of Jesus Christ

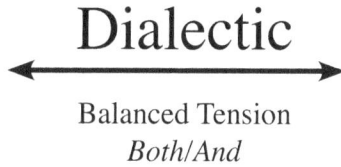

Dialectic

⟷

Balanced Tension
Both/And

Objective Universal	Subjective Particular
ALL	*NOT ALL*

Georg Wilhelm Friedrich Hegel
German philosopher - 1770-1831

"Marriage"

Book: *Philosophy of Right*, Pg. 167

Dialectic Contrast

←——————————————→

"Objective Universal"	"Subjective Particular"
Natural relationship	Ethical relationship
– physical bond of union	– psychological, spiritual bond of union
– legal bond of union	
– differentiated entities are bound together	– in mutual love the two individuals give themselves to the other
– "two become one"	**"What develops between these individuals may indeed be of infinite importance to *them*, but it is of no significance whatever in itself."**

The Extent & Efficacy of the Life and Work of Jesus Christ

Dialectic

$\longleftrightarrow$

Balanced Tension
Both/And

Universalism	Objective Universal	Subjective Particular	*Particularism*
	ALL	**NOT ALL**	

Objective Universal
ALL

ALL humanity loved by God

ALL humanity graced by God

ALL humanity elected in Christ

ALL humanity represented by Christ

ALL humanity died in Christ

ALL humanity redeemed in Christ

ALL humanity forgiven in Christ

ALL humanity reconciled in Christ

ALL humanity adopted in Christ

ALL humanity saved by Christ

ALL humanity has life in Christ

ALL humanity righteous in Christ

ALL humanity blessed in Christ

ALL humanity is "in Christ"

ALL humanity drawn to Christ

180

Subjective Particular
NOT ALL

We learn to live loved

We grow in the grace and knowledge

We are elect ones in the Elect One

we are united "one spirit" in Christ

We "reckon ourselves to be dead"

We live in the freedom of Christ

We accept God's forgiveness

We enjoy reconciled relationship

We cry "Abba Father! – adopted sons

We are being "saved by His life"

We affirm "Christ as our life"

We have become righteous in Christ

We have "every spiritual blessing"

We are "new creatures in Christ"

We draw near to the throne of grace

Subjective Particular

Biblical "theological anthropology"
- Tri-fold function
- Self-determinative function
  – "freedom of choice"
- Derivative function

Human response has NO merit.

Human response of FAITH
- Faith is a human choice-action
- Faith is NOT a "work"
- Faith is NOT a "gift of God"
- "Our receptivity of His activity"

Either-or Particularization

Indwelling Divine Presence
- Christ in the Christian
- Divine Spirit working in Christian
- Ontological exchange
- Outworking of Christ's life

182

Comprehensive Dialectic

← Balanced Tension →

Balanced Tension
Both/And

Objective-universal	Subjective-particular
ALL	***NOT ALL***
– God's sovereign activity	– man's response-ability
Indicative of God's action	*Imperative human response*
– grace	– faith
– God's work *for* us	– God's work *in* us
– effected/enacted by God	– experienced by believer
"Finished work"	*Process of salvation*
– historical/ theological	– experiential/ relational/personal
– representation	– relationship
You are included!	*You are intimately involved*
– collective humanity	– individual human beings

Philosophical and Theological Perspectives

Dialectic

←——————→

Realism	Personalism
Real objective existence in and of itself	Personal subjective choice and experience
Plato	Aristotle
Augustine	Thomas Aquinas
	Rene Descartes
Martin Luther John Calvin	
	Immanuel Kant
Hegel	
	Georg Hamann Soren Kierkegaard John MacMurray
Karl Barth T. F. Torrance (J.B.)	Norman P. Grubb W. Ian Thomas

Particularism

Objective Particularism

ALL is qualified to mean
   "ALL of God's predetermined elect"
- God has determined some
   individuals to be His "elect"
- God has determined other
   individuals to be "non-elect"

Subjective Particularism

ALL is qualified to mean
   "ALL individuals who subjectively
   respond to the gospel of Jesus in
   faith and in accordance with the
   acceptable religious prescriptions."
- It all depends on whether you do
   your part in the right way.

Calvinist
T.U.L.I.P.

T otal depravity

U nconditional election

L imited atonement

I rresistible grace

P erseverance of the saints

Augustinian-Calvinist
T.U.L.I.P.

T otality of human faculties rendered corrupt, depraved, deficient, and defective

U nconditional selection of certain individuals by a power-based deterministic deity

L imited extent and efficacy of Jesus' work – only for the predetermined "elect"

I rresistible action of God's grace to compel the "elect" to faith and impute/impose the benefits of Jesus Christ

P erseverance of the compelled "elect," disallowing permanent relapse and ensuring heavenly destiny

Universalism

←⎯⎯⎯ ⎯

General Universalism

ALL of humanity is designed and
destined to spend eternity in heaven
* This universal destiny has been
predetermined and is not predicated
on any human response.

Deterministic Universalism

ALL of humanity is deterministically
subsumed into the incarnational life
and ministry of Jesus Christ, and his
"vicarious humanity" incorporates
all human beings into His Being
and action for eternity.

Deterministic Universalism
T.U.L.I.P.

T otality of human faculties rendered
corrupt, depraved, deficient, and defective

U nconditional election of humanity in the
"Elect One," Jesus, by the power-based
deterministic deity

L imitless extent and efficacy of Jesus' work –
ALL humanity were substituted for in the
"vicarious humanity" of Jesus

I rresistible action of God's grace to compel
the "elect" to faith and impute/impose the
benefits of Jesus Christ

P erseverance of the compelled "elect,"
disallowing permanent relapse and ensuring
heavenly destiny

Deterministic Universalism A
ALL Humanity

... is integrally united with God – the separation of sin is but
an illusion of a depraved mind

... is subsumed into God's being in the union of deity and
humanity in the God-man, Jesus

... is drawn into fellowship and participation with the Triune
God via the humanity of Jesus

... is granted access into the Holy of Holies of God's presence
by Jesus who opened the veil in His flesh

... is replaced with the humanity of Christ before God. Jesus
was the "Man for all man"

... has been vicariously substituted for as Jesus was born,
lived, and died "in our stead'

... is baptized into Christ – overwhelmed into Him by His
assumption of our humanity

... is relationally "in Christ," i.e. has a relation with God by
the life and work of Jesus

... is a "new creature in Christ," for Jesus Christ has recreated
humanity in Himself

... has been transformed from being sub-human to being
Christ-humans – a Christ-replaced humanity

... has undergone an ontological exchange of being, nature,
identity & character in union with Christ

... is imputed with the entire character and being of Christ –
human being has become Christ-being

Deterministic Universalism
ALL Humanity

B

... is a Christ-instilled race – an ontologically altered race of human creatures

... became "partakers of the divine nature" when the divine-human Jesus became the redemptive integrator of God and man

... had the choice made for them, when Christ chose to become Man and live "as us"

... has exercised faith in God by the "faith of Christ" – Christ is the faith-er for all mankind

... is considered obedient by God, by the obedience of Jesus Christ in our place. Jesus is the "obedient One"

... prayerfully communes with God through the prayers of Jesus – Jesus is the pray-er for us

... worships God the Father through the worship of Jesus Christ – Jesus is the worshipper as us

... functions by the enlivening of Christ, for "in Him we live and move and have our being"

... functions by the provision of Christ, for "apart from Him, we can do nothing"

... has entered "eternal life" in Christ, and "are seated with Christ in the heavenlies"

... participates in the eternal heavenly destiny in Christ

... can disregard all the religious threats of hell – ain't no such place, and nobody's going there

God and

Divine Grace

General Universalism

All-loving inclusive deity

Non-responsive compliant humanity

Determinist Universalism

Power-based deterministic deity

Sin-limited deficient humanity

Grace-based relational deity
- revealed Himself in Jesus Christ
- reconciled humanity to Himself

A proper understanding of deity and humanity and the relation between them is essential to a proper understanding of the gospel.

192

Man

Human Faith

Free-choosing derivative
humanity
- capable of responding in
faith to God's grace-action
in Jesus Christ

***Objective
Particularism***

Power-based
deterministic
deity

Sin-limited
deficient
humanity

***Subjective
Particularism***

Law-based
demanding
deity

Self-directed
independent
humanity

Addendum S

THEOLOGICAL

Dialectic –

←————————

A human being functions spiritually,

←————————

Determinism

Deterministic causation
- diabolic determinism
- divine determinism
  - aka fatalism

The being and action of
human beings is
orchestrated and
manipulated by someone
or something outside of
the individual persons.
- Humanity is coerced into
a course of action, or such
action is imposed upon the
individual.
- Human beings regarded as
automatons.

Augustinian-Calvinism is
the primary theological
system that denies
human persons self-
determinative response-
ability toward God, and
indicates that God has
predetermined the
choices and actions of
human persons by
predestination.

A Derivative being

Human beings have *extrinsic* being, their
being is derived outside of themselves.

Humanity is eccentric, i.e. the center of
human beings' existence is outside of
themselves. No human being is an
"independent self."

Humans are *derivative creatures,* both in
origin and function.
- They do not exist *a se* - in themselves.
- They do not function *ek autos* - out of
themselves.

Human beings are personal beings, capable
of relating with the personal Creator, God.

Human function is dependent and
contingent upon a spirit-source, either
God or Satan (*ek Theos* or *ek diabolos*).
- Mankind is designed to be indwelt by the
Triune God, Father, Son, and Holy Spirit.
- From the spirit-source within, human
beings derive character, identity, image
and destiny by the receptivity of faith.

By means of derivation and dependency
human individuals express the character
of the spirit-source from which they
derive, in their spiritual, psychological,
and physiological behavior.

194

ANTHROPOLOGY

Tensioned balance

⟶

psychologically and physiologically as:

A Determinative being

God's Self-limitation of Himself avoids
absolute determinism, and provides for
a freely-chosen faith-love personal
relationship between God and humans.

Human beings have been granted the human
agency of "response-ability" – the ability
to respond to God and other humans.

With "freedom of choice" human beings are
free to choose or select the derivational
source and supply of their spiritual,
psychological, & physiological function.

This "freedom of choice" allows humanity
to exercise their human agency of
"response-ability" to respond to God's
action of grace to redeem and restore
humanity through the Person and work
of His Son, Jesus Christ.
- A response of:
 - personal rejection or
 - personal reception

Human choices have personal and
teleological consequences.
- the objective of an individual's existence
 and chosen behavioral expression is
 God's glory.
- Destiny and reward are consequences
 of human determinative choices.

Human Autonomy

The premise that human
beings are independent
autonmous beings, capable
of self-generating their
own character & activity.
- Human individuals are
"Independent selves"

"Free-will" is attributed
to human beings.
- the freedom to self-
determine one's actions
from one's intrinsic
being, and
- the freedom to self-
implement one's deter-
mined actions from
one's intrinsic power.

Such attribution of human
sovereignty is the core
of the philosophical
thesis of "Humanism."
- the theological form of
this thought is often
called "Pelagianism," or
sometimes questionably
identified as "Arminia-
ism."

What Changes?

Objective - universal   *Subjective - particular*

1	**No change** occurs collectively to the human race or individually to human persons, based on the historic advent, life, death and resurrection of Jesus Christ.	**No change** takes place within an individual human being, based on that person's response of faith to Jesus Christ, for they remain essentially a sinner until the final judgment.
2	**No change** occurs collectively to the human race or individually to human persons, based on the historic advent, life, death and resurrection of Jesus Christ.	A **definitive change** of condition and relation with God takes place within an individual human being, based on that person's response of faith to Jesus Christ.
3	A **transformational change** occurs collectively to the human race and individually within every human person, based on Christ's advent, life, death and resurrection.	A **cognitive change** occurs when individual human beings come to awareness with the faith of Christ to the objective-universal change in their essential nature.
4	A **redemptive change** is effected collectively for the human race, based on the historic advent, life, death and resurrection of Jesus Christ.	A **personal spiritual exchange** takes place in the spirit of an individual human being when they personally response with receptive faith to Jesus Christ.

WHAT CHANGES?

After perusing the four categories of statements represented in the foregoing diagram, the reader might consider:

- What are the theological differences in these statements?

- Is there an established theological community to which these statements apply?

- Which of these statements do you personally identify with most closely?

- What questions do you have concerning the differing statements?

This diagram was constructed after a reader who had just completed reading this book, emailed me with some questions pertaining to "what changes" occur collectively and/or individually to human beings in the objective-universal and subjective-particular categories of the gospel. After pondering his questions, I constructed the diagram wherein I attempted to accurately state four different viewpoints on the issues.

I will explain what I had in mind when I drafted the four variant interpretive options in the diagram:

No. 1 was intended to refer to the Classic Calvinist perspective. (*cf. Objective Particularism*)

No. 2 was intended as a generalized statement of modern Evangelicalism. (*cf. Subjective Particularism*)

No. 3 was an attempt to state the position of the Evangelical Calvinist. (*cf. Deterministic Universalism*)

No. 4 was intended to be a statement of a balanced biblical perspective as proposed in this book.

There will, no doubt, be those representing each of these perspectives who will object to the way their position is articulated in the categories.

Horizontal and Vertical Perspectives
of the Objective and Subjective Categories

Objective ~ *External*

Historical Foundation
Theological Formulation

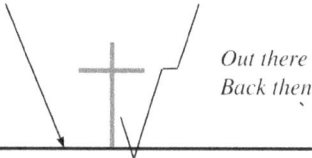

Out there
Back then

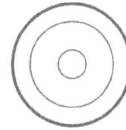

In here
Right now

Subjective ~ *Internal*

Personal Formation

Objective Universal ALL		Subjective Particular NOT ALL	
Adam	Christ	Unbelief	Belief
Fallen	Restored	"unbelievers"	"believers
Condemned	Forgiven	rejection	reception
Enslaved	Saved	Dead in sin	Born from above
Alienated	Reconciled	Hell	Heaven

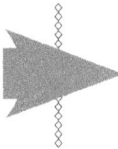

FINISHED WORK   *WHOSOEVER WILL*